# THIRTY AND TERMINAL:
## Cancer Survival

by

John R. Wagner

Seattle, WA
Infinity Publishing
1996

Copyright © 1996 John R. Wagner

All rights reserved. No part of this publication may be reproduced without express written permission of the publisher, except in the case of brief quotations embodied in critical articles or reviews.

Library of Congress Catalog Card Number: 96-78123

John R. Wagner

*Thirty and Terminal: Cancer Survival*

ISBN: 0-9651590-0-0

Editing & Production: Susi Henderson

*Back Cover Photo Courtesy of Yuen Lui*

First printing January 1997

10 9 8 7 6 5 4 3 2 1

Printed in the United States of America

# Dedication

To my uncle, Jim McGough,

who has prostrate cancer,

and who keeps me in touch with my father's family.

# TABLE OF CONTENTS

Prologue .................................................................... vii
Introduction ............................................................... 1
1   Childhood ............................................................. 3
2   Weddings One and Two ..................................... 11
3   Cancer .................................................................... 25
4   Coping With Cancer ............................................ 45
5   Outside Interest .................................................... 57
6   Rehabilitation ....................................................... 59
7   Resolutions ............................................................ 73
8   Parting .................................................................... 77
9   Freedom ................................................................. 83
10   Marriage the Right Way ..................................... 93
11   Winning the Lottery ............................................ 107
12   Conclusions…and Then? .................................... 111
13   Life Insurance ....................................................... 119
Interview with Dr. Nicholas Gonzales ............. 131
Appendix: Detoxification .................................... 139
Bibliography .......................................................... 149

# *Prologue*

Imagine the doctor sitting across from you has just said you have cancer. He then prescribes chemotherapy or radiation and recommends you begin immediately. When you raise concerns about toxic effects and the value of alternative programs, the doctor—with all his education, professional mannerisms, and certainty—tells you there is no scientific proof that alternative programs work.

This book is for all those in this dilemma, because it is nearly impossible to question or ignore the doctor's advice. The risk seems too great!

But does it always have to be an irrevocable, either/or decision? After evaluating the statistics in favor of the recommended treatment, you could choose one of the following: (1) Follow the doctor's treatment recommendation and either after or during this treatment, do an alternative program to help you detoxify and rebuild your body. The alternative program may believe chemotherapy or radiation is too toxic for their program, but that doesn't necessarily mean you might not benefit from it. *So if you're too fearful not to do the chemotherapy or radiation,* don't think you've given up your right to still pursue other methods. (2) Commit 100 percent to the alternative program, but after two months, monitor, through medical tests, the effect of your program. If you are unhappy with the results, feel free to change your decision. An alternative program should be demanding and comprehensive, and you should feel comfortable with the results. Never blindly trust assurance if it doesn't ring true to you, or test results that totally contradict what you're being told.

My approach was to leave no stone unturned in the ultimate battle. You must not hesitate to do everything possible to improve your chances for survival.

# *Introduction*

I was 23 years old, a law student at Detroit College of Law. My success was almost guaranteed. I was one of the best of American society. At least, this was what society and the social prestige of becoming a lawyer implied. Little did I know that I was, slowly but irrevocably, moving on a course that would lead to developing cancer—an experience which radically changed my life.

In my mind, people often fail to understand what in their life history and personality contributes to contracting cancer. I never suspected that some of my passive personality traits and lifestyle would bring me to the doorway of death. My hope is that by writing my story you can see, and therefore avoid, my mistakes and find ways to improve your own life.

# 1
## *Childhood*

I was nearly three years old when my mother left my father in California and relocated the two of us to Detroit to live with my grandmother. When my father came to attempt a reconciliation, my mother, who was already dating Don Wagner (whom she'd met on a blind date), refused. I will never forget the feeling of loss and helplessness I experienced when my father, John Robert McGough, said goodbye. At the time, I was jumping on the bed, holding my mother's hands, as my father stood in the bedroom doorway and said, "I guess I'll be going." I knew this was goodbye, and yet I did not smile nor acknowledge my father, much as I wanted to do so. I knew this was what my mother wanted, and being, naturally, closer to her than anyone else, I remained silent. Every time I think of this moment, I want to cry and to somehow change what I did that day and say, "Don't go. I love you, Dad." Naively, like that little boy, I still feel like this would have made a difference.

On that dismal, miserable day, I neither cried nor otherwise acknowledged my pain. Neither did my mother. We never discussed that day, and through the years there was an unspoken rule between us—we were not to discuss my father. I realize that, as a child, I learned never to do anything that would displease my mother, or she would instantly yell at me and temporarily withdraw her love. I learned not to invoke her disapproval. I was always careful not to make her angry.

In fact, my mother did everything she could to blot my father's existence out of her life. I'm told by my uncle and father that she refused to speak about her prior life or to attend any high school reunions. She would no longer meet her best friend from high school who knew my father well.

When she later announced that she would marry Don Wagner, I was very resentful; I had often made fun of him when they were dating. When my mother told me that I must call him "Dad," I emphatically said, "NO," but she just as determinedly retorted, "You WILL." She made her point clear with a hard slap across my face. The hatred I felt at that moment is permanently embedded in my mind. To this day, I have never been comfortable calling him

"Dad," as this seems too personal.

I knew he wasn't my father and I resented his presence. He interfered with the closeness I felt for my mother. Don Wagner adopted me, and I'm sure it was at my mother's suggestion. As a result of the adoption, my legal name was changed, and I'm told I had to be forced to write "John Wagner" instead of "John McGough." To this day, as I say my name, I feel uncomfortable calling myself Wagner. However, I will never change my name back because my stepfather did adopt and support me. He wasn't a bad father, just not a good father. He didn't know how to be a good father, as he didn't have one himself.

Throughout the years, I never had a close relationship with my stepfather. We were totally different and I was, as well, my mother's boy. However, he was never mean to me, and I never once felt he favored my two half-brothers over me.

My mother had two more children, six and eight years younger than I. This is when my mother's real frustrations began, when she was stuck at home with three children, because at that time my stepfather worked until 9:00 p.m. every night selling Oldsmobiles. My mother is not a mean person and can be lots of fun and totally charming. However, as she once related, she had a difficult childhood, with an alcoholic father who was very abusive to her mother. My grandmother, a sweet and most forgiving woman, would repeatedly leave her husband because of his abusive, alcoholic rages, and move back to Detroit from St. Louis. Her husband would sober up, come find her, apologize, and then they would return to St. Louis. This vicious cycle continued over many years until my grandfather was found dead along a railway track. Interestingly, my mother's older brother doesn't think of his childhood as traumatic, which leads me to suspect my mother was also abused and learned to blot out memories in order-to cope.

Given this background, it should not be surprising that my mother's relationship with my new stepfather didn't go smoothly. Every weekend and every Tuesday night, they went out partying and returned home very intoxicated. They would have the same fight every time. My mother would start it by accusing my stepfather of flirting with other women, sometimes accusing him of having affairs at work. She was very suspicious of his long work days. He never fought back, but instead tried to reason with her. This was unacceptable or insufficient for her, so she would raise the stakes by always telling him, "You tricked me into marrying you by pretending to have lots of money." (I often wondered if she regretted not reconciling with my father, her high school sweetheart, as she never obtained the financial goals she had hoped for.) Mother was never content until my stepfather was thoroughly upset. I always wondered why he accepted this treatment and I respected his patience. I concluded he really loved my mother.

This scene went on for years, and each time I would lie in bed crying, afraid to even go to the bathroom. The next day, the entire family acted like nothing had happened, though there was an obvious tension between my parents. We children understood we had better not talk about this.

When I started high school, my mother got a job. This wasn't a change for the better, as my mother became totally involved with her work-life and less interested in her children. I think this had a more damaging effect on my younger brothers, as they didn't get the attention younger children deserve and need. As for me, this was the time when I realized I wasn't as close to her as I had believed and hoped. When I sought her advice on a teenage problem, she'd criticize me, saying sarcastically that it was too bad or it was my fault. It was safer and easier not to talk to her and to act like nothing was wrong. She seemed tired from working and didn't want to spend the time with me.

However, if I acted pleased or didn't complain, and if I maintained good grades, I was rewarded with full use of the car. I lived a totally separate and mostly sufficient life, alone.

Mother and Father attended my youth football games (for 9- to 12-year-olds) and high school games, but afterwards I dreaded going home. I was the only one on the youth football team who for three years had to ride my bike to the field on game days, dressed in my football uniform—twenty long, cold, sometimes rainy minutes away—because my parents didn't like to go early. I never complained, I just accepted it; but I dreaded the bike ride home. My stepfather would be waiting for me so he could tell me, for a full hour, why I should have scored those two additional touchdowns. I just sat there and showed no emotion. But I felt rotten—I wasn't good enough for them.

However, they always stayed away from my high school baseball games and never asked the outcome. I had mixed feelings about this: sad because I felt alone and neglected, happy to not have to hear the inevitable criticism. In two consecutive high school years, I received a major sports award, and on both occasions, I was the only athlete unescorted by his parents to the awards banquet. The awards, which should have been a cause for celebration, seemed meaningless, as I had no one to share them with. There was no one there to be proud of me. I never revealed my hurt feelings, because to tell them would be to acknowledge my pain. I was well trained.

When I went to Western Michigan University, 150 miles away, it was because I wanted to be away from them. Even though I went to a great college preparatory school, I didn't even consider going to the University of Michigan, with its excellent academic reputation, because I had a lot of fear and doubts whether I could measure up to its high standards. Many of my high school classmates were clearly in the genius category, and I suspected everyone would be at this level at the University of Michgan.

While I was away at college, my parents and I seldom communicated. It seemed unnecessary and abnormal that my roommate received a weekly letter from his mother. I had no trouble being independent, given my childhood. My mother had always told everyone that we were a close family without any troubles. I never questioned this view nor even doubted that it was true.

This image seemed permanent. The good side of this upbringing is that I was very independent and capable of handling my own affairs. When it was time for me to start my own business, I had the strength not to need someone to rely upon. The downside of my independence and strength was my lack of preparedness to be close to other people or to handle my own relationships, as the future proved.

I don't mean to say that my childhood and my home life were totally rotten. Far from it. However, it was a life that failed to nurture or develop some aspects of emotion, expression, and intimacy in me. This had, I believe, an impact on my later development and my health. But on other levels, there were many happy days and good things my parents did for us. My mother had a great sense of humor and was generally easygoing. There was no physical abuse in our family, and I know the negative aspects were unintended consequences of my parents' own difficulties.

In retrospect, my mother deserves full credit for one decision she made that put me in a position to succeed and grow. She had me attend, at an additional expense, an elite, all-boy Catholic high school, De La Salle Collegiate, where 99% of all graduates attended college. There I had to do at least two hours of homework every night, starting in my freshman year. Report cards were issued every two weeks with a comprehensive quarterly exam after eight weeks. By the time I graduated, I knew how to study, take notes, and pass any exam.

When I began college, I was amazed by the undisciplined and unorganized students, and how easy classes were. I started to suspect that maybe I was smart. Even in law school, I only studied eight hours a week until the final two weeks of each semester. I had become a professional student and test taker because of my high school education. Of course, along with higher learning comes exposure to ideas; that provided stimulus for self-improvement and growth. I owe this to my mother's decision to seek the best education for me.

In very many ways, she was doing the best she could, particularly given her own background.

# 2
## *Weddings One and Two*

In 1973, I was living in a ghetto in Detroit, Michigan, in an apartment building whose residents were ninety percent homosexual. My monthly rent of $150 was split with my roommate. We had a view of the neighborhood's main street, Grand Boulevard, where daily we could watch purse snatchings occur below us. My yearly income at the time was only $2,000; but in order to obtain financial aid for law school, I had to misrepresent my financial statements to show additional income. The financial aid advisor had informed me that no one would believe I lived on only $2,000 per year and that I should show a minimum income of approximately $3,500.

In spite of my living conditions, I was in law school, satisfied with my life, and I was sure that I was in control. After all, I had succeeded in being admitted to law school, had avoided the altar, and thus far had managed to support myself. I wanted to live my life my way. A product of the sixties, I rejected many traditional American values. Marriage, for example, was anathema to me. I had little respect for the institution, not ever having seen a marriage where the partners acted like they loved each other. After all, who wants to live in an institution? Major corporations, whose only goal was to make billions regardless of the consequences, also drew my ire.

My only complaint was that all my college friends lived near Kalamazoo, Michigan, 150 miles away, where I had been an undergraduate at Western Michigan University. Upon my return to Detroit, I discovered that, as a graduate, I suddenly had difficulty meeting women. At the local bars, all I met were secretaries or clerks who immediately asked what I did. If I said I was a law student they were very interested in me. But usually when I said that I was unemployed, it immediately halted any interest. To make matters worse, I always broke the first rule by not buying them a drink. I questioned why I should buy them a drink when I didn't even know them. I wanted a woman of substance, one who would appreciate me, not how much money I had nor what I was going to do. Perhaps I was too cheap.

As an undergraduate, I had always had girlfriends, so now I was unhappy with my nonexistent social life. I missed the company of a steady girlfriend. What intimacy I had in life came from having a girlfriend I could do things with. I didn't have good, close, male friends, as I didn't know how to get close to males. Women were less threatening, and there was sex and what passed for intimacy. And of course I sought intimacy without commitment, since I had learned never to trust anyone one hundred percent.

These were the circumstances under which I met Eva, an Austrian woman traveling through the U.S. on vacation. Eva was travelling with a girlfriend who knew my roommate, and one morning I awoke to find her sleeping on my couch. I was in my second year of law school. Her uniqueness appealed to me. She didn't speak fluent English (though she had a beautiful accent) and hadn't grown up watching American television. She wasn't the typical American girl my parents would have wanted for me.

In that one week she was in Detroit, Eva and I began a romance. I was fascinated with this European woman whose goal wasn't owning a house in the suburbs and two cars—just a simple, happy life. She didn't think in terms of materialistic goals. Being a law student didn't mean much to her, since a law degree was the easiest professional degree to obtain in Austria. Eva's lack of respect or admiration for traditional American values was perfect. We exchanged letters and I went to Europe for a total of three months over the next year to visit and travel with her. We travelled to Florence, Rome, and Vienna, and even attended a Viennese ball, where we danced to the strains of Mozart.

During this time we talked about and began to plan for her to come to the U.S. to live after she graduated. I said nothing to discourage these plans at the end of my two-month summer trip, even though I had inwardly begun to have doubts and misgivings about our relationship. I dismissed these as homesickness and decided to see how I felt after I returned home. But returning home to my lonely social life only encouraged me to overlook any doubts. This, of course, enhanced our relationship. Eva became the focus of my dreams, and my fantasy made it easy to proceed with our plan to live together. I had rationalized that I wasn't making a commitment, so we could use living together as a test of our relationship in a more conventional setting.

Then I encountered a major problem. American laws regarding noncitizens did not permit her to live in the U.S. without marrying an American citizen—obviously me. I, who had fought successfully to stay single in the past and had ended two long-term, solid relationships rather than get married, was faced with giving up my precious freedom. There were doubts in my mind about our relationship, but I was a sixties person. If I wouldn't let them send me to Vietnam, I especially resented the U.S. government telling me I couldn't live with someone. So we decided to get married, secretly, and between us act as though it hadn't happened. In other words, we would "live together," even though we would be legally married.

We took part in a civil wedding for 40 couples who were simultaneously married by a judge in a large auditorium. All the couples lined up to repeat the vows together. I kept silent. The whole scene made me feel like I wasn't really getting married at all. The judge couldn't resist making fun of the newlyweds, reciting the traditional vows with sarcasm. Not surprisingly, both of us were depressed after the ceremony, but for different reasons. We never discussed it in depth, but I felt like I had done something I didn't believe in. Eva, on the other hand, was disappointed because she had wanted a *real* marriage. I tried to comfort her by telling her that if we continued to successfully live together we would have a real marriage later that year.

Six months later our relationship was still drifting along satisfactorily, so I agreed to a Christmas wedding in Vienna. We never sat down and actually *discussed* whether we should get married at all, let alone in a church ceremony with her family present. Still, I consented to a wedding because I knew it would make her happy and because I felt obligated—even though I still had deep reservations and really didn't want to get married. I believed I could never meet someone who would arouse feelings in me so strong that I would willingly give up my freedom. In other words, I thought this was the closest I'd ever get to the feeling of total love, and that this was probably a "normal" male feeling. I did make one thing clear, however; I didn't want to make any vows that would make me feel like I was actually getting married. I wanted our relationship to remain as though we were just living together, uncommitted.

With hindsight, I can see that what I wanted was impossible. *How could I get married for her and stay unmarried for me?* It was naive and credulous of me to think this was even a possibility. When we arrived in Vienna for the ceremony, this slowly and painfully became clear.

Once in Vienna, I discovered that my mother-in-law, Maria Schmutzer, had arranged a church wedding complete with minister and vows. I had wanted a simple state ceremony without formal vows, but when I started to voice my concerns to Eva, she became extremely upset. I realized a church wedding was important to her. So I withdrew my protest, thinking that since I was getting married for her, I should give in on this one point.

The next day, after I had given in to the church wedding, I was told by Eva that we had to meet with the minister to obtain his approval of our wedding. I was outraged, of course, that I had to obtain a minister's approval, and that Eva—and her family—expected me to say all the right things to satisfy this man. At that time in my life I was definitely *anti*-formal religions; but again I gave in to her wishes and went to the meeting, although I emphatically stated that I would not lie about my beliefs. Luckily for my mother-in-law and Eva, the minister didn't speak English, and he only questioned Eva as to how we would raise our children. To my way of thinking, children were not in the picture, as I had no picture of "family."

After this meeting I was once again angry at myself for doing things I didn't believe in, but I didn't know how to stop the momentum of their carefully arranged (without my knowledge) events without calling off the wedding and hurting Eva deeply. Hurting Eva was out of the question, even though I didn't want to go on with this formal ceremony.

To make matters even worse, my relationship with Eva's family, especially her mother, was highly uncomfortable. For example, even though her family spoke English, we frequently ate an entire meal with only German spoken. I felt disturbingly uncomfortable, especially when Eva neither translated their conversation for me nor encourage them to speak English.

Eva's mother informed me that Austria is the

country with the most culture in the world. The only time, for example, that English was spoken at a meal was when Eva's mother told me that Americans have no culture and no formal language, as American English is not a language. "A good example of your lack of culture," she said, "is that you do not constantly hold your silverware in both hands while eating your dinner, like we Austrians do." (She didn't appreciate my response that this was only so they could east faster.)

It became glaringly obvious that I had a traditional mother-in-law relationship—and I wasn't even married yet. My only retaliation was when she asked me about my good German name ("…although German is not as good as Austrian"). I told her my parents were not German and that I was actually part American Indian. This abruptly ended all discussions about my heritage. She never took the least trouble to inquire about, let alone to understand my pride in my Indian background. It was too much for her to consider that her cultured Austrian daughter could marry an American Indian (one small victory for me in the mother-in-law battle).

As we awaited our wedding day in this warm, friendly atmosphere where no one spoke to me, there were other things that I did contrary to my wishes—like buying wedding rings. I told Eva I was opposed to wedding rings, but she wanted them so I consented angrily. As with most of our decisions, we didn't discuss them, and I held my resentments tightly inside, wondering how she could so blithely ignore my desires, not even considering them. For me, rings were just too traditional.

When my wedding day came, I wasn't happy, but I resolved to get it over with so I could get out of Maria's house. To be in an environment with a lack of communication is taxing enough without the overt hostility that was manifesting itself. My emotional rollercoaster ride went from anger to depression, and my resignation continued until one hour before the wedding, when Eva told me that her mother had just tried to persuade her to change her mind. I knew I was in enemy territory.

So, ironically, though I really didn't want to go through with the ceremony, I resented Eva's mother trying to end it. I perceived it as another insult hurled my way. In one small way, it made me want to follow through with it—the result of my little war with Maria.

You can imagine my response when, immediately thereafter, Eva told me her mother wanted Eva's brother, Gerheart, to be my best man (though I had given no thought to the requirement of the best man). None of my family or friends from Detroit had come, but I was determined not to be attended by Eva's brother, who seldom spoke to me and was jealous whenever I spoke to his attractive wife.

So I selected Evelyn, a high-school girlfriend who lived in Munich and had come to Vienna for the wedding, as my best man. This was the highlight of my day; it gave me a sense of doing something my way, nontraditionally, and totally opposed to Maria's wishes. Of course, she now felt I had rejected her son in favor of a woman as best man, and this further illustrated my lack of culture and class. *Americans!* (And another small victory for the good guy!)

As for the ceremony, conducted by the minister in a traditional manner, it had one saving grace. It was in German and all I had to do was say "Ya" at the appropriate time. At least I didn't have to listen to all the words and vows I didn't want to be bound by. Like the first wedding ceremony in Detroit when I didn't repeat the vows, I clung to the belief that this meant I wasn't really getting married. The most depressing aspect of the ceremony, (even though I didn't want to acknowledge I *was* getting married) was that when I looked around, I didn't have any family or close friends present—except my best man, Evelyn. I felt lonely and rejected because my family wasn't there, because they didn't have any valid reason not to attend my wedding. (They had no idea that I didn't consider this a real wedding.) Only Eva's family attended. Their hostility manifested itself again at the end of the ceremony. As we were leaving the church Eva's grandmother frowned and bitterly growled to Eva, "You finally got what you wanted." Whatever happened to congratulations?

Walking outside, I felt relieved that it was finally over, but when we jumped into her father's car I realized this was just wishful thinking. Eva's mother jumped in the back seat with us and for the next 40 minutes talked nonstop to Eva on the way to our reception. I stared out of the window feeling entirely alone, wondering how Eva could let her mother continue to ruin every detail. My wedding had just ended and my feelings toward Eva were not of love, but anger, as I listened to her mother's nonstop voice.

For the remainder of the evening, at the reception, I hardly spoke to Eva because her mother talked to her continuously. I wanted to explode with the anger, resentment, and pent-up emotions I had firmly restrained and controlled for the last ten days. When Eva and I were finally alone in our room, she made it clear that she didn't want to hear my feelings and was expecting a traditional wedding night. So I complied, acting out feelings I didn't have. Afterward, I lay in bed, empty and alone. I didn't understand that this was my fault, and trying to blame Eva was simply a venting of my own frustrations.

Furthermore, I had married for all the wrong reasons. I was foolish to believe I would never deeply want to get married. Not only did I not understand nor recognize my own emotions, but I lacked a positive vision of marriage, families, and love. My goal was not to end up like my mother and her marriage. Unfortunately, I had no clue how to accomplish this, and I didn't even know I was clueless.

It was also wrong for me to do things I didn't believe in just because I didn't want to hurt Eva's feelings, or her mother's. Obviously, neither Eva nor I were much good at expressing our feelings, and our relationship continued to follow the patterns we had established: she was the emotionally weak and dependent female and I the strong, decision-making male whom she depended on. I would seldom express my true feelings, as I knew she didn't want to hear unpleasant thoughts—just like my mother. When I was upset I would bottle up my feelings; I would become extremely quiet and distant, and she would leave me alone and not inquire into my behavior. My withheld emotions turned into resentments, for I wanted someone who would notice my silence, which indicated a need to talk. Eva ignored this silence, and the gulf between us grew. Only by talking about our true feelings could we overcome our difficulties, but neither one of us would break out of the code of silence. I wanted desperately to talk, but something in me wouldn't allow it. I didn't recognize my obligation to speak but rather, felt it was her obligation to inquire. This perception kept us trapped in our vicious circle.

Eva seemed oblivious to my overt signs. I wondered how she could be so blind. I lost respect for her, and this disrespect only increased when her mother was around, because Eva would never stand up to her, permitting Maria to treat me very poorly—a rerun, it seemed, of the wedding experience. Our relationship had established patterns which didn't allow us to obtain true intimacy, and only resulted in further alienation. Our lack of communication left us poorly equipped for the stresses that awaited us.

# 3
## Cancer

Eva and I returned from Vienna and tried to return to our previous lifestyle without speaking about the marriage. We were somewhat successful, but the bad taste of our unpleasant wedding lingered in the background, and we did nothing to alter the noncommunicative patterns we had established.

I graduated from law school, and after going door-to-door looking for a job, I was finally appointed the City Assessor of Hamtramck, Michigan. Hamtramck is a small city of approximately two square miles in the middle of Detroit, a Polish community. This job led to my appointment as a part-time Assistant City Attorney six months later. My outstanding qualification for this position was the city's residency requirement for its employees, and I was the only attorney in Hamtramck interested, or desperate enough, to take this job.

These positions provided a good education into grassroots politics and graft. One incident which occurred while I was City Assessor should illustrate. A furniture store owner came to me and told me about his excellent relationship with past assessors. The basis of the relationship was that in exchange for a favorable assessment, he would allow me to obtain furniture at unheard-of prices. My reaction was to order a full audit of his store which resulted in his assessment and taxes increasing more than what I would have originally assessed it. I was insulted that he believed I could be bribed.

The advantage of the City Attorney position was that it also allowed me time to pursue a limited criminal private practice in Detroit. All I had to do was sign up with the circuit court and they would regularly assign me to defend indigent defendants. There I experienced how the system really worked. Most of my cases involved drugs, and when I interviewed my clients they would always claim to be innocent and detail how the police physically abused them when they were arrested. At the preliminary hearing, the police would deny this, and lie about why they stopped and searched my client. The police were very good at it because they knew if they admitted they didn't have probable cause to stop my client, the case would be thrown out. The net result was that my clients were physically abused, but they were guilty and usually had no defense. So I would plea bargain and they would plead guilty to a lesser charge. Justice was done.

Therefore it should make perfect sense that one-and-a-half years later we moved to Seattle, Washington, because Seattle was everything Detroit wasn't. It had a mild climate, was clean and beautiful, and had little crime. Unfortunately, what Seattle had too much of was attorneys, so my only job offer was as a law clerk for $2.50 per hour in Tacoma, a city 30 miles south of Seattle. I was very discouraged and felt my only choice was to start my own law practice. I tried to get court assignments to defend indigent defendants but there weren't many criminal cases in Seattle. The couple of assignments I received showed Seattle police to be much more honest.

In one particular drug case, I asked the state patrolman why he had stopped my client. His reply, that he had "just had a feeling," was shockingly honest, and the judge had to dismiss the case for no probable cause to search my client. In Detroit, the police officer would have said that my client was swerving all over the road and when they stopped him, he threw something out the window (presumably drugs).

Unfortunately the sharp contrast between cities didn't help me find work. I wondered how I could survive in my own practice.

To complicate matters, much to our surprise, Eva had gotten pregnant prior to our departure. Eva's doctor had told her she couldn't get pregnant as her tubes were blocked, and we naively had trusted the doctor. (Of course, my explanation was "super sperm.")

We handled the pregnancy like all else. We didn't discuss our fears and anxieties. When our daughter, Maria Theresa, was born, neither one of us was prepared to handle the stresses the child placed on our relationship.

We were living in a one-bedroom, 600-square-foot basement flat, and Maria's crib was in the twelve-foot-long hallway between the bedroom and the living room, next to the bathroom. Three weeks after her birth, Eva's mother came to stay with us. She gave us approximately three weeks' notice that she was coming to stay for three months. She slept on our couch in the living room, twelve feet from our bedroom door.

Needless to say I resented her presence in our tiny flat; Eva's and my relationship reached a new low. I became angry with her mother and her for not allowing me to care for Maria, as she constantly attended to her. As a new father, unsure of how to care for a baby, I held back my objections. I was not confident in my new role, so I unwillingly submitted to her control.

This control also continued at meals, where she would dominate the conversation by constantly speaking to Eva in German. Whenever I spoke, she would immediately switch to German as soon as I paused. Eva and her mother would constantly be together with Maria, and I felt completely excluded. When I brought this to Eva's attention, she just shrugged and said that "maybe" she would talk to her mother. Again I was disappointed in her for not standing up for me.

At this time our communication became even worse, and it only deteriorated further when we went to bed. When the doctor gave Eva permission to resume sex, I was shocked by Eva's total lack of interest. I wasn't aware of a woman's normal lack of sexual interest after childbirth, and I had incorrectly presumed sex would return to the prebirth level. When I tried to discuss my frustrations with Eva, she wouldn't respond; instead she would fall asleep. I found this frustrating, as I felt shut out of both their lives. I would lie there, angry and bitter. Adding insult to injury, I would wake up and find her mother on my couch.

I experienced that same feeling every day when I returned home from my yet-unsuccessful law practice. I felt like there was an invader in my space. Eva's mother and I did not even attempt direct communication. If we had anything whatsoever to say to each other, we would speak through Eva as a translator.

Furthermore, I didn't have sports as an outlet for my frustrations, as I had a leg injury that kept me from my regular tennis and soccer schedule of three times a week. All my tensions were totally bottled up inside. The only improvement over the next year-and-a-half was Mother Maria's return to Austria. There was little discussion of problems, and I often went to sleep angry and resentful.

I finally recovered from my leg injury and began playing soccer in the best amateur league in Seattle. At 30, I was still the fastest on the team. I could run three miles in 18 minutes. I believed I was in great physical shape. I didn't pay much attention to a slightly pulled back muscle that I noticed in March, 1980.

Two months later, in May 1980, I got sick with a flu that lasted two weeks. Usually, whenever I had the flu it lasted three or four days, not two weeks. When I recovered I noticed that the pulled back muscle had returned, but I attributed it to my recent lack of exercise. However, when I started to exercise, the pulled back muscle became a more severe back pain. In fact, the more I exercised, the worse it became. So I tried rest, but the pain didn't go away, it just continued to worsen.

I even took the extreme step of going to an osteopath—a medical doctor who is trained, like a chiropractor, in back manipulation. Dr. Thresler performed some manipulations (or adjustments), but they only made my back worse. At one point, he diagnosed my problem as one leg being half an inch shorter and prescribed a shoe insert to equalize my leg length. All I knew was that the pain was steadily increasing. It progressed to the point where I could not even lift Maria, now two years old, without severe pain. So the osteopath sent me to an osteopathic surgeon because he was concerned about my fourth lumbar vertebra, which had white spots in the x-rays. Initially, he had dismissed these spots as gas showing through from my intestines. (Some gas!) Since, I wasn't improving, though, he felt this vertebra should be examined.

The osteopathic surgeon had no better luck diagnosing any obvious reason why I was having back pain, but he was suspicious of my vertebra with white spots and wanted to know if I had ever had any prior x-rays so he could determine if this was a preexisting natural condition (for me) or evidence of something amiss. He went so far as to suggest that there was an outside chance of cancer. I wasn't totally surprised at this suggestion, because I had begun to suspect a serious problem. My concerns were only somewhat allayed when the results of a bone scan seemed to indicate that my vertebra wasn't cancerous.

My doubts still lingered, because I was not improving; and although the doctor had indicated that I didn't have cancer, he hesitated and said that the bone scan wasn't quite as conclusive as he would have liked.

Nevertheless, I tried to trust his diagnosis and follow his advice of rest. My condition stabilized somewhat until about two weeks later, on July 2, when I made a quick move and felt a searing pain run down my leg. The pain was so intense I shouted out and almost cried. I limped to bed and discovered that once I was in bed I couldn't move off my back to either side without a searing pain that shot up and down my left leg. The only position that gave me some relief from the pain was with my knees up in the air, my feet flat, drawn up towards my butt.

The pain was so severe that I couldn't leave the bed to go to the bathroom, and whenever I fell asleep I would wake up screaming when my legs relaxed and slipped from the upright position. I phoned the doctor and he said that this condition is caused by nerve pain and inflammation of the sciatic nerve, and that after a few days (to perhaps two weeks), it normally improves. So I laid in bed, terrified, and hoped it would suddenly improve.

On the second day, I was determined to ignore the pain and go to the bathroom. It took me 15 minutes to slowly sit up on the side of the bed. When my foot finally touched the floor, I screamed at the sudden agony; I doubled up and fell back onto the bed. The pain was shooting up and down my legs for what seemed like hours (but was probably only five minutes or so). My knees were up and I pushed my foot as far as possible to my butt, hoping it would stop. As it slowly eased off, I trembled and shook with the subsiding pain and the terror of not knowing what was wrong with me. I was afraid to even turn my head from side to side. I even was afraid to phone the doctor.

Finally, five days later, on Thursday, unable to sleep or eat because I was afraid of having to relieve myself, I phoned the doctor. Dr. Thresler, the osteopath, who had not come to examine me even though his office was only two blocks away, decided on the telephone that I should go to Waldo Hospital, an osteopathic facility. It was July 7, 1980, and I felt like I was in the middle of a nightmare that had started two months ago and from which I couldn't wake up. The worst thing was that it seemed like the nightmare was just beginning, with no end in sight. I was abysmally frightened.

During this time, I didn't see much of Eva, since her aunt was visiting and she was also self-employed part-time. As it happened, when the aid car came she wasn't home. I felt very alone. When the aid car attendant tried to pick me up and move me to the stretcher, the same searing pain went through my body and I reflexively lashed out with my hands and scratched the attendant's face. The force of my strike drew blood and caused this trained attendant to drop me, which initiated an even greater pain. It took half an hour for this pain to subside and for them to figure how to lift me. Luckily, they had an eight-inch wide, six-foot long board in the aid car, which I was able to slide onto over the next 30 minutes. Then they lifted this board onto the stretcher. During the time I was scooting onto the board the attendant was constantly complaining that I was too slow and if I didn't hurry up he would move me. I had to constantly beg him to give me more time.

At the hospital I was placed in a bed on my eight-inch board because I refused to move off it, fearing they might want to move me. There was no way I wanted to endure that pain again. When the nurse came in she tried to raise my bed. When she raised it too high, the bed suddenly collapsed back to the lowest position. This was the second time I had been dropped that day, only this time it was worse since I landed on the board. My scream was so loud that two nurses ran in to see what happened. When I could finally speak, about ten minutes later, I told them about my condition. I yelled at one nurse to stop when she attempted to again raise the bed.

During all the time I was in that hospital, I rarely saw a nurse; they seemed hesitant to enter my room. My request for pain killers was denied, because my doctor had forgotten to prescribe one. Even though I was surrounded by doctors, none of them would help me because I wasn't their patient.

Twenty-four hours later, the osteopathic surgeon who had examined me three weeks earlier appeared. He said that I was his patient now, and not the osteopath's who had sent me to the hospital, and that he would have x-rays taken on Monday. It was Friday, and the x-rays couldn't be scheduled until Monday. So I had two long days to think, lying on my board.

When Monday finally arrived, they took x-rays which confirmed that my vertebrae were unusual. The radiologist (who analyzed the results), told me that I had a growth on my vertebra with a 50-50 chance of being cancerous. I was horribly depressed.

It wasn't until the next morning that the osteopathic surgeon returned. He said that there was little likelihood of cancer, especially since I was 30 years old and in good physical shape. He believed that I probably had a cracked vertebra. I felt better, but I was still concerned because of the conflicting diagnoses. He recommended a transfer to Swedish Hospital, under the care of a Dr. Gunn, who was supposedly the best in the West for cracked vertebra surgery. He said he would make the arrangements. He also persuaded me that I could move off the board, as it wouldn't be as difficult to move me, now that I was in a hospital bed. This was Tuesday.

On Wednesday, my sixth day in the hospital, my doctor returned for five minutes to say that I would be transferred the next day to Swedish Hospital under Dr. Gunn's care. I questioned him about the delay, but he said that wasn't unusual.

On Thursday, the eighth day I had been in the

hospital, thirteen days since the searing pain had begun, I was transferred to Swedish Hospital. I was very happy to leave Waldo Hospital, as it had been a very depressing, lonely experience. I hoped that a new hospital would end my anxiety of not knowing and fearing the worst.

I had been left almost entirely alone, as my room didn't have another patient and the nurses seemed hesitant to enter. None of my friends visited until the last day, as Eva had not told anyone I was sick until I questioned her about their whereabouts. The only thing on television was the Republican National Convention. Eva was busy taking care of Maria. Even though she explained why she couldn't visit much, I still felt very hurt—if she were sick I would have found a way to visit her every day.

Friday morning I met with Dr. Gunn. He immediately recommended a myelogram so he could get a better view of my spinal canal. Unfortunately, the test couldn't be run until Monday. Dr. Gunn preferred to wait until the next week, as it was his opinion that the best personnel have the weekends off. So, like Waldo Hospital, the world stopped on the weekend except for my thoughts, which kept racing. I now had another 48 hours to lie in bed, without moving, to speculate and worry about whether I had the dreadful disease.

When Monday morning came, I was ready for the myelogram, a test I'll never forget. It began with an injection for relaxation one hour before. It was essential to be relaxed, because the test involved the insertion of a needle at the base of the spine. This needle was hollow so that they could place a needle within the needle to inject a dye into my spinal canal. Then when the dye was inserted, the table I rested upon was raised and lowered to various positions and angles (resulting in some unusual diagonal positions) while the technician took x-rays. This terrified me; I feared I would be placed in a position which would trigger the nerve pain, causing me to double up and forcing them to stop the test or to sedate me. Or worse yet, cause the needle to break off. It took about 40 minutes to complete the test. (Luckily, the worst didn't happen, and I was greatly relieved when I was finally back in my hospital bed.) To top it off, I had to lie totally flat without a pillow for the next 24 hours while the dye passed out of my system. If I didn't lie totally flat I would develop a "spinal headache" which, I was told, was to be avoided at all costs.

Of course, my results weren't available for another 24 hours. When Dr. Gunn received the report—it was Wednesday, 20 days after the searing pain had begun—he told me that my problem was a herniated disc, and that a bone fusion operation for a cracked vertebra wasn't required. This was good news, because a herniated disc operation is much easier on the body. I asked about the growth that had been previously reported at Waldo Hospital. He said that it appeared to be a benign cyst that they would look at in the operation; but that the odds were only one in 100 that it was cancerous. As for my pain, Dr. Gunn said that my disc was protruding significantly enough into my spinal canal to cause the nerve pain I experienced. So, feeling somewhat encouraged, I awaited the operation (which of course, couldn't be scheduled until the following Monday so that I could have another few days to lie in bed and speculate on my future).

When Monday came, I was so frightened I considered walking out of the hospital. I wanted to believe that everything was okay, because my nerve pain seemed to be gone, although I hadn't been out of bed for three weeks to test it. The time for the operation came. All I remember is trying to prolong a conversation with Dr. Gunn, when the world suddenly went black. Afterwards, I remember waking up in the recovery room believing I was dead. Never before in my life had I been unconscious without a feeling of being alive. I didn't even dream. For a long time I trembled at the recollection of this total blackout.

After the operation, Dr. Gunn came by to pronounce the operation a success. They had removed a growth coming out of my vertebra that was entangled with some nerves. He said that he was sure it was noncancerous, but that the results of the bone biopsy would not be known until Thursday.

After the operation, I was very groggy and received

injections for pain approximately every three hours. On one occasion, in the middle of the night, an elderly, overweight nurse came in to administer the injection. Not only did she mistakenly jam the needle into my hip instead of my butt, she also knocked my IV out. It took her ten minutes of poking my hand to find my vein. My pleas for her to leave me were ignored. I complained to the head nurse and much to my surprise she agreed that this woman was incompetent. The head nurse explained that this nurse couldn't see very well and often had problems with patients. However, since she was two years short of retirement, no one wanted to fire her in spite of her incompetency. That was a nice gesture by the hospital but I wondered about the patients who needed help and didn't get it. (Aren't there other jobs for nurses that don't involve patient contact?)

When the morning nurse came in, she asked me whether I wanted an injection or pain pills. I asked her why I suddenly had this choice. She said that I always could have elected pain pills over injections. Of course, no one had previously mentioned this option. I suspected that the patient is usually the last to know about his choices.

The day after the operation, I started to again suspect that everything wasn't normal. The nurses started collecting my urine for a test they suspiciously said they didn't have any information about. In addition, I was not allowed to get out of bed, even though prior to the operation Dr. Gunn had stated that the day after I could get up and start rehabilitating. Suspicions were again growing.

Two days later I knew why they had collected my urine and confined me to bed. It was Thursday, at 6:00 p.m., 28 days after the searing paid had begun, and the CBS evening news with Walter Cronkite had just begun. Dr. Gunn, who looks a bit like Walter Cronkite, entered my room looking like someone had just died. He said that the bone biopsy showed a cancerous tumor which had been confirmed by the urine test. It was a cancer of the bone marrow called myeloma. He said that my chances had been one in 100 of having cancer, since this type of bone cancer rarely occurred in people under 50. This wasn't the lottery I wanted to win.

I was totally shocked. I wanted to cry but couldn't. I didn't know what to do. I asked myself, "Why me?" and the doctor, "How long do I have to live— three months, one year?" Dr. Gunn didn't know. He referred me to a cancer specialist whom he said would come the next day. So I had to wait again—one more long, long day— to know how soon I would die and what, if any, my options were.

For a long time I just stared into space. When I finally phoned Eva, I felt she was too weak emotionally to handle my cancer, so I painted an optimistic picture rather than telling her how I really felt. I acted as though this was a minor problem and she seemed to take it very well. When I hung up I still remember feeling so alone and wishing that there was someone in the world I could turn to for help.

    The next day, Dr. Weber, the oncologist (cancer specialist), came to my room and explained my cancer to me in a manner very different from the sketchy report given by Dr. Gunn. Dr. Weber explained that this cancer could be either solitary myeloma or multiple myeloma, depending on the number of places it appeared in my body. The distinction was important, he led me to believe, because there was a 30 percent chance solitary myeloma wouldn't reappear; whereas multiple myeloma was incurable. Furthermore, death wasn't always immediate, as myeloma was a slow-growing cancer of the bone marrow. (Most people discover they have multiple myeloma when they unexpectedly break a bone).

    To determine if I had a multiple myeloma, Dr. Weber had two tests conducted—a bone scan, which is a type of x-ray, and a bone graph, which turned out to be very unnerving. For the bone graph, the doctor first numbed the area around my right hip. Then, using a drill, he slowly bored a hole into my hip. The object was to obtain a sample of my bone marrow to determine if the cancer was prevalent throughout my body.

    Four students were observing the test and the

doctor commented to them that everything was going exceptionally well and that although he already had a good sample he could probably get "an extra long one." At this point I wasn't thrilled with the sound of the drill going into my hip and his desire to get "an extra long one." I requested that he stop since he already had a good sample. He stopped. I'm still amazed at how often people are abused in hospitals unless they continually speak up and question every procedure performed on them.

Another example of hospital abuse is the two interns who came into my room on different occasions. They both told me that Dr. Gunn had requested that they examine me. They had me move until I triggered the nerve pain. These exams by the interns were the only times I experienced pain while being examined in the hospital. Finally, after asking Dr. Gunn if he had sent anyone to examine me, I discovered that these interns had misrepresented themselves so they could practice on me. I still cringe at all the pain and discomfort interns inflicted on me without my consent, under the pretense of being sent by my doctor. I requested that these interns not be admitted to my room.

That afternoon the results of the two tests disclosed that the myeloma was only in my fourth lumbar vertebra, which meant, as Dr. Weber had led me to believe, that I had approximately a 30 percent chance that the myeloma wouldn't reappear. After being told I had cancer and expecting to die only 40 hours earlier, 30 percent sounded very good. (At this time, I didn't know that this 30 percent was not accurate, and that all known studies concluded that solitary myeloma always becomes multiple myeloma.) I was allowed to leave the hospital the next day, but only after they placed me in a body cast that ran from under my armpits to slightly below my hips. Dr. Gunn wanted to protect my vertebra (which was soft from the cancer) from sudden movements that could cause it to crack, with unfavorable consequences. The cast would keep me from making sudden moves.

Before I left the hospital, Dr. Weber arranged for me to begin radiation therapy two days later, on Monday morning. This would be the first of a total of 28 treatments, Monday through Friday. (The world still stopped on weekends.) The theory behind the radiation therapy was that a sufficient dose would be administered each time to kill a majority of the cancer cells and 50 percent of the normal cells. The normal cells, however, would regrow very quickly and replace the cancer cells. Twenty-eight treatments were necessary to ensure all the cancer cells were killed. The success rate was 99.9 percent; but this only pertained to the myeloma in this vertebra; not the 70 percent chance of its recurrence somewhere else in my body.

When I was checking out of the hospital I was given two forms to sign. One was a large computer printout verifying all the treatment and medication I had received (as if I'd know) and the other, a promissory note for all of my bills. As an attorney, I know that a promissory note entitles the hospital to win a lawsuit easily and collect all their attorney fees and court costs. This may not sound unusual to the layman, but an individual in a lawsuit is not automatically entitled to his attorney fees and costs even if he wins, unless there is a signed agreement, like a note which so specifies attorney fees and costs, or a state statute providing for all fees and court costs to be paid by the losing side. Otherwise, attorney fees and costs are totally up to the judge's discretion. So even though I intended to pay the hospital, if I *didn't* repay promptly the hospital could initiate a lawsuit and include its fees. I wondered about the people who couldn't afford to pay promptly or whose insurance company delayed payments? Furthermore, if I wanted to contest their charges on the computer printout, it would be more difficult because I signed a promissory note. So, of course, I refused to sign the note.

The hospital staffer told me in a hostile tone that I had to sign or I wouldn't be discharged. I smiled and told them that I was leaving and asked if she would prefer that I go back upstairs to my room? After conferring with her supervisor, she irately told me I could go. Otherwise, I could have written the story of the man who never returned home because he couldn't, or wouldn't, sign the hospital form. Free room and board. What a thought.

# 4

# *Coping With Cancer*

Finally I went home, after 25 days in the hospital, wearing a body cast and diagnosed as having a 30 percent chance to live. I was thoroughly depressed and confused. I wondered how long I would live and how I should live my life. Dr. Weber had said that if the cancer became multiple myeloma I could still live ten years with treatment; he wasn't really sure. Fortunately mine had been discovered in the beginning stages, so I probably had some time. Nevertheless, the fact remained that I had cancer, and I didn't know how to live.

On Monday, two days later, I returned to my law office. I was self-employed, just a one-man law office. There are no sick days with pay for the self-employed. My office was in turmoil. I had lost a lot of business because of my five-week absence, but I didn't really care. I had cancer and was concerned with life and death, not money. I stopped doing any promotional work as I had in the past. I was satisfied with whatever business found me, which amounted to about two hours a day of work. I sat alone with my thoughts for my remaining hours at work.

On that same Monday morning, I went for my first radiation treatment and was instructed to wait in the patients' waiting room. All of them looked like the stereotypical cancer patient—sickly, pale, skinny to the bone and many in wheelchairs. It was so depressing to think that I could become like them that I returned home feeling little hope and wholly depressed.

That night I phoned Dr. Weber to ask more questions about myeloma. I wanted to know and understand everything so I could be prepared for the worst. Surprisingly, he persuaded me that it wasn't a good idea to study myeloma. He felt that the literature only dealt extensively with the 70 percent who had recurrences, describing how the myeloma had spread, rather than dealing with the 30 percent who survived; he said there was little to write other than that they survived. He didn't want me to dwell on the negative aspects, but rather on the positive. Furthermore, when I told him that I didn't feel comfortable around all those other patients in the waiting room, he said he would arrange for me to wait in the general public's reception area so that I had minimal contact with other cancer patients. I quickly accepted his advice and suggestions, as I had always thought I was a positive person. I believe Dr. Weber's advice was the best thing he did for me. It helped me fight against the bleak picture of being a cancer victim with only expectations of death.

The fact that people get what they expect became vividly clear the next day. I went to a cancer counselor at Swedish Hospital. I told her that I was interested in self-help and wanted to fight against cancer. She recommended two books, *Getting Well Again*, by Carl O. Simonton, Stephanie Matthews-Simonton, and James L. Creighton and *Anatomy of an Illness*, by Norman Cousins.

I immediately went to a bookstore and bought the Simonton book. What I read astounded me. Previously, I had associated cancer with a short life expectancy followed by death. It was encouraging to read that the recovery rate from all cancers was 50 percent. Furthermore, Dr. Simonton, a radiation oncologist, was a medical director of the Cancer Counseling and Research Center in Dallas, Texas, where he had pioneered an holistic therapy working with incurable cancer patients. His program had a survival rate of double the national norm and in 20 percent of the cases, total remission.

Dr. Simonton's theory was based upon a model which suggested that cancer begins with psychological stress leading to depression and despair which cause the limbic system to record this message and influence hypothalamic activity. The hypothalamus is a small area off the brain which participates in controlling the immune system and the pituitary gland, which itself regulates hormones in the body. When this area is affected, the immune system is influenced, causing a decrease in the body's ability to fight abnormal cell growth like cancer. In addition, the pituitary gland is affected, producing an imbalance in the adrenal hormones, and resulting in the increased production of abnormal cells (cancer). In other words, stress can weaken the body's immune system at the time it needs it most—when it is most likely to produce abnormal cells.

What Simonton's technique attempts to do is reverse this process by having the patient call upon his immune system to fight cancer. This is done through a visualization technique which requires that the patient to learn how to totally relax and then visualize—create a picture in his mind—of his white blood cells attacking, destroying, and removing the cancer cells. Interestingly, when the patients who were not having much success drew their visualization, their drawings would show only a few white blood cells attacking hundreds of cancer cells. Simonton reasoned that they could never get well if they believed their chances of success were overwhelmingly slim. When Simonton worked with them to change their visualization by adding white blood cells, they would begin to achieve success. (It's not surprising to me that many cancer patients have difficulty creating a positive visualization, since their doctors have told them they will soon die. Such encouragement can't help anyone's recovery process.)

When I began to visualize, I had no difficulty seeing thousands of my white blood cells attacking a few cancer cells and removing them from my system. (I was predisposed to a positive approach and determined to succeed.) This technique gave me both a feeling of fighting back and confidence that I could battle cancer and win. I directed all my thoughts and energies towards believing I would win.

One reason I was following this technique was that I had already questioned why cancer returned in many cancer patients. The general theory—that the surgeon didn't get it all, or the treatment wasn't one hundred percent effective—*didn't ring true for me.* I suspected that the cancer treatments, with all the poisonous chemicals, are usually effective and kill the cancer; but the patient's body, which initially produced the cancer, could well do so again unless *something* changed. Therefore, I questioned whether there was something wrong in the way I was living, for I feared that if I didn't make changes, my body would produce cancer again.

When I questioned my oncologist and the radiologist about this theory of the cause of cancer, they provided no information or opinions. They gave their usual answer that there were no scientific tests proving the causes of cancer. It was only in Simonton's book that I found some guidance as to the physical and psychological explanation of cancer.

One of the most interesting things Simonton refers to in his book is the "psychological process of illness," which identifies five steps that frequently precede the onset of cancer.

1. Experiences in childhood result in decisions to be a certain kind of person.
2. The individual is rocked by a cluster of stressful life events.
3. The series create a problem with which the individual doesn't know how to cope.
4. The individual sees no way of changing the rules about how he or she must act and feels trapped and helpless to resolve the problem.
5. The individual puts distance between him- or herself and the problem because of a static, unchanging result.

As to the first step of the psychological process, which revolves around experiences in childhood and decisions to be a certain type of person, Simonton states that all of us remember when our parents did something we didn't like, and we made an internal pledge never to be like that or never to behave in a similar way. In my case, not only had I, at a very young age, unconsciously developed my code of silence to obtain my mother's approval, my parents had those many evening fights every week when I was a child. As I lay in my bed crying, wondering why they fought so often and whether they were getting a divorce, *I resolved never to quarrel, even if it meant suppressing emotions, because it could not produce a favorable outcome.* (I didn't even realize this rule was consistent with my childhood decision to please my mother at any cost.) I followed this rule in all of my relationships and as a result, I internalized all my bad feelings and built-up resentments. My wedding was an excellent example.

Another resolution made during my adolescence was *not to express my true feelings unless I was totally convinced someone was listening and demonstrating a strong desire to know how I felt.* In other words, a person had to pass a strict test— that they didn't even know existed— before I would confide in them. I made this decision because whenever I expressed to my parents my personal feelings, or ideas that were important to me, they only offered negative comments and said that, at my age, I couldn't have problems. Furthermore, I was convinced my problems weren't important to them, since they never remembered from one day to the next what my concerns were. In fact, I tested them periodically by telling them conflicting stories about the same event on successive days. They never remembered I had said exactly the opposite just 24 hours earlier. They never listened to me, so I felt there was no reason to express my feelings because I didn't think they cared.

These decisions were important because they limited my ability to handle stress, which left me unprepared to cope with the second step in the process—being rocked by a cluster of stressful life events. In the two years preceding my cancer I experienced the following:

|     |                                            | Points |
| --- | ------------------------------------------ | ------ |
| 1.  | Sexual difficulties [after the pregnancy] | 39     |
| 2.  | An addition to the family [Maria]          | 39     |
| 3.  | Business adjustments                       | 39     |
| 4.  | Change in financial status                 | 38     |
| 5.  | Change in number of marital arguments      | 36     |
| 6.  | Mortgage over $10,000                      | 31     |
| 7.  | Change in work responsibilities            | 29     |
| 8.  | Change in living conditions                | 25     |
| 9.  | Revision of personal habits                | 24     |
| 10. | Trouble with boss                          | 23     |
| 11. | Change in residence                        | 20     |
| 12. | Change in recreational activities          | 19     |
| 13. | Change in social activities                | 18     |
| 14. | Change in number of family gatherings      | 15     |

These stresses are from a Social Readjustment Scale, developed by Dr. Thomas H. Holmes of the University of Washington, that assigns values to stressful events. My stress list was compiled according to this scale and totalled 400. Holmes found that 49 percent of people who had accumulated scores over 300 points within twelve months reported 90 percent more illness than did people in the bottom third.

Step three in the process of illness is the creation of problems caused by stressful events that the individual doesn't know how to deal with. In my case, my relationship with Eva seemed beyond my control, and although it wasn't perfect before, it had only gone downhill after the birth of Maria. In addition, I felt the financial pressure of having to support my family with my new business. I was unable to cope with these stresses because of those rules I had created for myself about withholding my feelings. Therefore, I held in all these stresses, which caused me to accumulate even more resentment.

This fits in perfectly with step four—the individual feels trapped—because I didn't see any way of changing the rules. With Eva, divorce was out of the question because it would be irresponsible, and because I couldn't bear the thought of hurting Eva or detrimentally affecting Maria. So I felt helplessly trapped, with no control over my life. My decision as a young man to be a certain type of person didn't provide me with a way out of my problem. As Simonton puts it, I saw myself as the victim because I couldn't resolve my problem.

Regarding step five, Simonton notes that the hopeless victim sees serious illness or death as a solution. In my case, I felt helpless, without any hope of improving my relationship; I was not consciously aware that I saw illness as a solution. However, as Simonton states, this process doesn't *cause* cancer, but permits it to develop by interfering with the body's immune system, which causes changes in the hormonal balance and leads to an increase in the production of abnormal cells.

Now that I had an understanding of the psychological processes, I had an idea of how my psychological health had contributed to my getting cancer. I resolved to bring about changes in myself and my environment and not to repeat my errors. Just resolving to bring about change gave me a sense of hope. Even though I didn't know exactly how to change my life overnight, I was determined to slowly work on my problems and believed I would find the way to happiness.

My first priority became my physical self, which was encased in a body cast, fighting against cancer. In addition to using Simonton's visualization technique, I had started reading books on nutrition and self-healing. My relationship, which was a major problem, wasn't my first priority, because I knew I didn't have the physical or emotional strength to directly confront the problem. Instead, I resolved to slowly seek improvement in my relationship by trying to be more open and by discussing my thoughts with Eva.

Unfortunately, whenever I attempted to discuss my thoughts and ideas, Eva was unresponsive. Whenever she reacted in this manner I felt rejected, lonely and disappointed. I didn't realize that she also had to make an adjustments to my cancer—that living with a cancer patient had to have been a threat to her lifestyle.

A good example of our lack of communication and misunderstanding of each other occurred one week after I came home from the hospital in a body cast. Eva asked me (indirectly, of course), "Why don't you want to have sex?" I was astounded that she didn't realize that I was still in shock, afraid of dying, and that sex was the last thing on my mind. Now I realize this might not have been a selfish act, but her way of reaching out for help. Nevertheless, I hungered for a compassionate friend.

# 5
## *Outside Interest*

Six weeks later I discovered the compassion which had been missing in my life. A new client came in to the office—Judy, who was blond, attractive, 28 years old, and very sensuous. She noticed that I was in a body cast and inquired as to my illness. She was very sympathetic, as she knew about chronic pain from her own ongoing back problem. In addition, she was knowledgeable about nutrition and alternative healing techniques. This meeting led to lunch and eventually to an affair that lasted two months. During this time I felt a forgotten passion and a closeness that had been missing in my life. I had found an ally with whom I could spend hours discussing my health problems.

At the time, I told myself I didn't want Eva to know, though I now believe the opposite. I would come home occasionally at 7:00 p.m., three hours later than usual, and say I had been working late. When Eva spoke to me, I would hardly speak because I felt such resentment at having to come home and leave Judy. Eva seldom questioned me about my strange behavior. I respected her even less for not reading the signals I was sending her. Nevertheless, I didn't leave her; I ended the affair at the height of its passion. I decided not to leave Eva because I thought I might be overreacting to all I was going through. I wanted to be fair to Eva and be sure our relationship couldn't improve before I ended it. I resolved to renew my effort at improving our relationship and painfully tried to forget the other woman.

# 6
# *Rehabilitation*

Eight weeks after getting out of the hospital, I had my first checkup. I was greatly relieved when my blood and urine disclosed no cancer proteins. It appeared that the radiation therapy had been successful, although there was still a 70 percent chance it would recur in another part of my body. However, I'd passed the first checkup and now had three months more to live until the next one, although for cancer patients there isn't a day that passes without the thought that some headache or other body ache is cancer. I also had my body cast removed. I was elated until I looked in the mirror and saw my hip sticking out to the left. Dr. Gunn said it was from back muscle spasms, but I could begin to play light tennis. In spite of Dr. Gunn's opinion, I had reservations about this recommendation, since I had just recently started to walk normally. Nevertheless, I played a game of tennis because I wanted to play so badly, and because my trusted doctor had given his permission—he was a *back surgeon*, after all!

Playing tennis was a mistake, even though I only played for ten minutes. By the time I got home I had severe back pain and spasms. I hadn't listened to what my body told me and now I was paying the penalty. I had chosen to believe the doctor was right, and that he knew my body better than me. It had never occurred to me to weigh my doctor's advice against my own inner feelings. (My mother had always told me, "Listen to the doctor and do whatever he says.")

When I phoned Dr. Gunn, he prescribed muscle relaxers, but they didn't help. As a result, over the next six weeks I was compelled to lie down whenever possible but I didn't improve, despite Dr. Gunn's assurances that rest would solve the problem.

When I went back to him in December, he seemed more concerned about my problem. He scheduled a CAT scan (an extensive x-ray) to determine the source of my continual pain and suffering. When the results of the test came back, there were differences of opinion. The x-ray technician, whose job is to diagnose these scans, concluded that there were cells in my lumbar vertebrae consistent with myeloma (cancer). Dr. Gunn felt that cancer could explain why I was having pain. He said that, in comparing similar cases, he had never seen a vertebra respond as slowly as mine in producing new bone mass. Furthermore, he recommended a bone fusion operation in which he would take out the fourth vertebra and replace it with bone from my hip.

Dr. Weber, my oncologist, didn't agree with these opinions, as he found it difficult to believe that myeloma could survive the radiation therapy. He believed that since my blood and urine test showed no evidence of cancer, the cells showing on the CAT scan could be dead cancer cells.

I was again profoundly depressed and wondering if I could ever wake up from this nightmare. I felt I had suffered enough, yet the end didn't appear close at hand. I had started to focus on how much the doctors didn't know and I found it disturbing that they made recommendations in spite of their ignorance. They admitted that x-rays only show shadows and these shadows could be dead cancer cells as well as active, growing ones. They weren't sure, yet they considered a major surgery to remove my vertebra because they expected to see new bone growth. They decided to wait six months and retest. The last thing Dr. Gunn told me was not to engage in physical activity because my vertebra had not filled in with new bone mass and it could crack, causing a more severe condition.

When I left the doctor's office, I was relieved that the latest stress was over for six months and depressed that I might still have cancer. I resolved to try to rehabilitate myself. After seven months of listening to doctors, my physical condition was severely handicapped, and I realized the doctors were only guessing about what a specific test showed.

So I started to devise my own physical rehabilitation program. I began going to a swimming pool and sauna three or four times a week. At first, I could only walk one lap of the pool; any swimming would result in severe back pain. When I could finally swim one length, I'd try for two and then three. Somewhere in the process I would go too far. My back would go into spasms and I'd have to start all over again at the walking-only stage. This rehabilitation was very frustrating, because one day I would feel elated, having swum another length, and the next day depressed, because I had to start over again and slowly work up to my previous point. I was always questioning whether I'd ever return to good physical condition. Nevertheless, after four months of persevering, I was swimming up to 20 lengths without having any back spasms and I was beginning to feel physically fit once more.

Simultaneously, I resolved to make dietary changes. In October, two months prior to the great debate on whether I still had cancer, I had started going to health food stores to read about nutritional approaches to cancer. I had begun to study nutrition because I believed in Simonton's theories, and it seemed a logical extension of his views that nutritional deficiencies could play a role in weakening the immune system. It seemed that Simonton had neglected this area and I was determined to research it, so that I left no stone unturned in my battle with cancer. (I wondered whether Simonton was afraid that if he included a nutritional approach, his book would be rejected by the medical establishment.)

The nutritional information and theories I read about were astounding to me, since I was raised with little nutritional education. Some of the facts that first caught my attention were as follows:

1. The RDA (recommended daily allowance) and MDR (minimal daily requirements) were established by politically appointed boards, whose members were connected with the dairy and meat industries. (How naive of me not to realize politics is everywhere.)

2. That the AMA (American Medical Association) statistics show that vegetarians live, on average, seven years longer and have fewer incidents of heart attacks and cancer.

3. That cancer cells thrive in sodium solutions but die in Vitamin C solutions. The average American

consumes seven grams of salt per day. The daily requirement is less than one gram.

4. Our bodies, unlike those of other animals, neither make nor have the ability to store Vitamin C. A glass of orange juice, which is advertised as supplying so much Vitamin C, has only *one tenth* of a gram.

As a result of all the reading I did and my frustration with the lack of help from my doctors, I put together my own rehabilitation diet and program. As I saw it, there was nothing to lose. The first things I did were:

1. Stop eating all red meat.

2. Stop eating salt and any products that contained salt (which excluded 90 percent of everything in a typical food store).

3. Stop consuming sugar and white flour.

4. Begin taking: 25,000 I.U. Vitamin A
10,000 I.U. Vitamin D
100 Milligrams of Vitamin B
5,000 Milligrams of Vitamin C
1,200 I.U. Vitamin E

After I made these dietary changes, there was a period of about ten days in which my body adjusted to the changes. I had diarrhea and didn't feel as super as I thought I should. Then I suddenly experienced a breakthrough and felt better than I ever remembered. I continued going to the health food stores, and I read everything I could find on nutrition and cancer. I found the recurring theme in all holistic books to be that, in order to achieve health, the body must be detoxified of poison and simultaneously supplied with the nutrients necessary to rebuild and replace the unhealthy cells. In other words, a person's immune system can be stimulated to rid itself of cancer through diet if given the proper assistance.

This theme fits in with Simonton's mental and emotional approach. There was one book that seemed to encompass all of the other books. It was *A Cancer Therapy* by Dr. Max Gerson. Dr. Gerson's basic premise is that all cancers result from a toxic liver. The liver's function, as the largest organ in the body (approximately one-and-a-half feet long), is to filter out impurities and poisons. If it is unable to function properly cancer will result, as the body is prohibited from producing healthy cells and the immune system is overtaxed. Therefore, Gerson believed that the liver had to be detoxified to eliminate the poisons in the body. To do this, he prescribed the drinking of fresh fruit and vegetable juice every two hours and coffee enemas at least twice a day. The theory behind the coffee enema is that the caffeine is absorbed through the intestines into the gall bladder and liver, which then stimulates the liver to excrete toxins. He believed that this procedure had to be followed for one-and-a-half to two years to totally replace and rebuild all the liver's damaged cells.

When I first read about this procedure and his remarkable results I believed in its success, but couldn't imagine how I could ever take an enema. It sounded gross and painful. But one day, I was in a health food store looking at Gerson's book, when a young lady said to me, "That book really works." I asked how she knew, and she said that her mother was given up as an incurable cancer victim 15 years ago and that she was still alive today at 65 after going on the program. Furthermore, she added that her mother belongs to a local cancer society, composed of members with similar stories. When I told her my story, she warned me that if I didn't undertake a detoxification program that I stood a great risk of cancer returning.

Her story about her mother had been so convincing that her warning was the final push I needed. I was convinced I had to follow Gerson's program, even though I dreaded the idea. So I bought bottled water and coffee and proceeded to try. To my surprise, I discovered that it didn't hurt to insert the enema, that I didn't have any waste leakage, and that I could hold the coffee inside me the required ten minutes to allow the caffeine to be absorbed. In fact, after the third enema I learned to relax and do Simonton's visualization while I held the coffee. I always felt great afterwards and, as a result, looked forward to my morning and evening enemas. It gave me a strong feeling that I was really fighting back.

Notwithstanding that Gerson's purpose is not to cleanse the intestine, but to detoxify the liver, I believe these enemas have this dual effect. Many health food books are written on the benefit of cleansing the intestine, and this could be another reason Gerson had success with his program. Other authors note that cancer victims do not have regular bowel movements of at least once a day, and they recommend colonics for their cancer patients. They ask the question, "If we have three meals a day and have less than one bowel movement per day, where do all our waste products go?" This is a question each of us should ask ourselves. Norman Walker, in his book, *Diet and Salad*, illustrates the healthy and unhealthy colon, and the difference is outstanding. Walker believes that most diseases result from a congested colon.

The second part of Gerson's program involves drinking fresh vegetable juices made from organic vegetables every two hours. This part of the program was much easier to implement. (Thank God.) I bought a Champion juicer and proceeded to drink between 40 to 60 ounces a day of vegetable and fruit juice. I chose a Champion juicer because I had read test results showing that the Champion model was the only juicer under $200 that produced success for cancer patients. The theory as to why the other juicers didn't produce good results was that when the juice is made it is spun too much, allowing oxygen to get in, thus causing oxidation, which changes the juice's electron balance from a positive to a negative.

Two-thirds of the juices I drank were vegetable juice and all of them had carrot as a base: carrot-celery, carrot-celery-parsley, carrot-apple, carrot alone. I never would have believed how sweet carrot juice can be, if good carrots are used.

The advantage of fresh vegetable juices drunk within 15 minutes of production is that the enzymes, which die quickly, are still alive. Thus, I was drinking a live, vibrant food which could restore and rebuild my liver and body cells. In other words, I was eliminating toxins through enemas and providing live food to rebuild my damaged cells.

The benefits of this program were soon very apparent. After six months I noticed that my eyesight had improved and I no longer needed to wear the glasses that I'd worn since I was 18 (though I didn't have terrible eyesight to begin with). I had an eye exam and found my vision had returned to 20/20. In addition, I stopped getting colds, which I had always had at least twice a year, and, when I did have the flu, it was truly a 24-hour (or less) flu. Considering that I had accepted colds and three-day flus as a part of living, I was pleased that nutrition and attitude could so greatly alter my health.

Another ailment which disappeared was a daily

eyeache I had since I was 18. Proper nutrition alleviated the problem. I wondered how many of us accept these little ailments as natural, not knowing they can be eradicated though nutrition.

Also, since I had been a teenager I had experienced a lot of mucus in my system. This was evidenced by the frequency with which I cleared my throat and felt the need to spit (much to the displeasure of some of my girl friends). Upon experimenting, I noticed that when I eliminated milk from my diet for about three weeks, my mucus would disappear. This was extremely difficult for me to accept since I loved milk and drank six glasses per day (with my cake and other desserts). I had always felt comfort in the belief I was consuming a very healthy product.

Not wanting to accept these results, I conducted my experiment over and over by drinking milk for three weeks and then eliminating it. Each time, after three weeks of drinking milk, the mucus would accumulate and I'd start clearing my throat. The mucus only went away when I discontinued milk. Reluctantly, I accepted that milk was mucus-forming and that I definitely felt better without it. It was difficult to let go of my faith in milk. However, my experimenting is consistent with the research on cows' milk. Cows' milk has an enzyme, casein, which is 300 times greater in concentration than in mothers' milk—and it is used to make airplane glue. As I think about it, it makes sense now that cows' milk is more mucus-forming, since cows' milk is intended to grow a 2,000-pound animal.

Some people may argue that if we don't drink milk we have to be careful to consume the RDA of 65 grams of protein per day. Who determined that we need 65 grams of protein per day? It couldn't be the dairy and meat associations, who make sure their friends are appointed to the RDA committees and who distribute free charts to schools showing the basic food groups and the amount of each we should consume—could it?

Finally, when I returned for my checkup six months after the doctors had wanted to do major surgery, they decided that the new test suddenly showed evidence of new bone growth and that I didn't have cancer and I didn't need an operation. Of course, I already knew this. When I proudly told them what I had done, the doctors just smiled and said that this would have happened anyway and that there is no evidence that nutrition had any great effect. However, they did admit that belief could have contributed to my cure.

I was shocked and disappointed by their attitude and their unwillingness to acknowledge the contribution of nutrition. I began to wonder if it could be that they, as doctors, only believed in what they had studied and refused to acknowledge that a person could cure himself without their help. Nutrition isn't consistent with prescribing drugs, and I discovered that the average doctor has less than one course on nutrition in medical school, and much of doctors' updating is furnished by drug companies that also sponsor research.

I continued the Gerson program for approximately one-and-a-half years, though I did reduce my enemas to one per day after six months. Gerson believed that the liver, the largest organ in the body, takes one-and-a-half years to totally rebuild itself. My physical health continued to improve. Six months after I had begun my rehabilitation program, I was able to play tennis for one-and-a-half hours, every other day.

# 7

# *Resolutions*

During the period of my rehabilitation, I also began to alter my attitude toward living. One of the resolutions I made was that I would live each day as though it were my last. I realized for the first time in my life that I wouldn't live forever and that there was no reason to postpone any dreams. So I made plans to do things I had always wanted to do, beginning with climbing Mt. Rainier, one of the largest mountains in the continental U.S., at 14,410 feet. It was a two-day climb which required sleeping at a base camp, 10,500 feet high. I signed up with the Rainier Rangers, who gave all the climbers a one-day climbing workshop. On Memorial Day, 1982, I proudly stood on the summit of Mt. Rainier, approximately one-and-a-half years after the doctors had said that I needed another operation. It was a satisfying feeling.

I continued with my resolution to do all the things I'd always wanted by taking my backpack and flying to London to go to Wimbledon. A tennis junkie, I had always dreamed of being at center court for the finals. When I departed for Wimbledon, eight days before the finals, I was determined to somehow get in, despite being unable to get tickets in advance. Much to my good fortune, I discovered upon arriving at Wimbledon that ten rows from the court along the sidelines was the unreserved standing room section, which was actually a better place to view the games than most seats. These standing places were so sensational that you could almost reach out and touch the players and all for the cost of approximately $6.00.

What did it matter that I had to line up 18 hours prior to the gates opening, sleep all night in line, and then—when the gates opened at 1:00 p.m.—race and push to get to the standing room before all the places were gone. The experience was totally enjoyable. The time in line went quickly, as there were people from all over the world and the atmosphere was charged with excitement and anticipation. It was enjoyable to watch the dignified English people suddenly lose their control, fighting to gain a place in the standing room area. As an American, I had a definite advantage in the fighting department, as I had no dignity to protect. So of course, I always got the front row and was privileged to watch some of the classic tennis matches of all time. Borg v. McEnroe, Final 1982; Borg v. Connor, Semi-Final 1982; Connor v. McEnroe, Final 1983.

After my first Wimbledon, I met my good friend Vince from Detroit, and we traveled to Germany to see Evelyn, my best man. (Before we rendezvoused with Evelyn, Vince and I had such a spectacular time in England that it is best described only in our memories.) After the German meeting, I went alone to Denmark, Norway, and Sweden, fulfilling another lifelong desire to backpack in Europe. In fact, my trip was so overwhelming that I repeated it in 1983.

Prior to having cancer, I never would have allowed myself to go on these trips, as I would have felt guilty leaving Eva and Maria. However, I finally realized that if I didn't go, I would regret it my entire life; that there was nothing wrong with doing things for myself. Furthermore, these trips allowed me time to be on my own so that I could reflect on continually improving my life.

One thing Simonton said in his book is that cancer can be the excuse a person needed to do things he otherwise would not do. This seems appropriate, since prior to cancer, I was unhappy with my life and didn't know how to change it. I would never have gone on these trips. I resolved never again to need cancer as an excuse to do the things I really wanted to do.

## 8

## _Parting_

After returning from Europe in 1983, I knew it was time to work on letting out all the deep resentments I held within me. Simonton, Gerson, Chinese medicine and other literature I had studied all report cancer victims are people who carry around deep resentments and anger. The Chinese believe that each of the five emotions—anger, grief, joy, fear, and worry—is stored in a different part of the body. The liver is where anger and resentments are stored. This is consistent with Gerson's theory that a diseased liver causes cancer. In my case, I had lifelong anger and resentments towards my parents and Eva. I felt the time had come to deal with them.

I knew that I wanted to release my anger towards my parents. I didn't know the best way to do it, so I first turned my attention to Eva. I began by telling Eva that I believed our relationship had evolved such that I was the strong male, and she was the weak female who was overly dependent on me; I needed, I told her, someone who could be my friend and listen to me. She felt hurt and defensive, but she didn't disagree with my analysis.

Periodically, over the next six months, I'd attempt to tell Eva about my resentments and about Simonton's theories and how they related to me. She would listen but never have much to say. When I mentioned improving our relationship, she was very noncommittal. I felt like I was forcing the issue upon her. As a result, this attempt at honesty and communication didn't change our relationship very much; I felt better, but often the discussions resulted only in Eva feeling hurt. Accordingly, we would quickly fall back into our old patterns. I was discouraged that our relationship was not improving. I still felt the need to continue to let out the resentments I had bottled inside me, yet we just didn't seem able to talk about them. That was sad, because I discovered that when I discussed my feelings, I would feel better, regardless of whether we arrived at a solution. Just discussing anxieties made them seem less important.

To be fair to Eva, I should mention that she also had great difficulty discussing feelings as a result of her childhood and, perhaps, her Austrian heritage. When Eva was still very young, her father began an affair with another woman, with whom he has lived for 30 years without divorcing Eva's mother. What was most uncomfortable for Eva was that her father kept his business in her mother's apartment, so every day her father came there to work. They would have lunch together as a family, and there were always angry discussions between the parents. One can only imagine the effect this environment can have on a child. Eva's self-esteem was never promoted or encouraged, and she had a very poor example or foundation for communicating or handling disputes. I believe she also made the decision when she was young that it was better to avoid disagreements.

So we never learned to discuss our problems; when I once brought up my unhappiness with our sex life, which was as much my fault as hers, I hurt her very deeply. She had felt the quality was satisfactory and took this as a personal insult. I felt sex should be a means of establishing a spiritual connection, and I thought we needed more openness and growth in technique and expression. This was one of the last straws in our marriage. In the remaining four months we lived together, we never felt comfortable with intimacy.

When I decided to go to Europe again in June of 1983, I felt that our relationship was more honest than it had ever been and for that reason it was better. However, I was far from satisfied.

That year I flew to Greece from London and, while on the island of Nikos, I met a German woman walking along the village street. She had long, blonde hair, a beautiful tan, and she had been living with her boyfriend for nine years, as I had with Eva. She had a son, was a vegetarian and believed in natural healing. Needless to say, I was elated to meet someone with whom I felt I could totally relate. For the next nine days we shared a very special experience.

Parting was very painful, as we both were returning to our mates; we never discussed the possibility of meeting again. We merely exchanged addresses and both wondered what would happen when each of us returned home.

In the days before I returned home, I did some serious thinking. I concluded that my relationship with Eva was adequate, but that it could never come close to fully satisfying me, and if it didn't satisfy me it couldn't possibly satisfy her. If I were still living with Eva in 30 years, I knew I would feel disappointed that I didn't have all I could have had in a relationship. It didn't matter whether I would ever see the German woman again, but I knew I would rather be free and risk always being alone, so I could have the possibility of finding true love, rather than stay in a relationship that was only adequate. In addition, I concluded that it would be better for my daughter, Maria Theresa, to have the opportunity to observe a relationship based on a fulfilling love rather than having our relationship serve as her example. I realized how much my childhood example had affected me, and I didn't want her starting with the same limitation.

Eva and I had met and formed a relationship when I was very different. Since then I had gone through cancer, recovery, and rehabilitation; my attitudes, needs, and goals had changed. Sadly, we were not able to grow together. So three years after having had cancer and after having attempted to improve our relationship, I moved out.

# 9

## *Freedom*

It was a great feeling of freedom—free of regrets, because I had made sure prior to leaving that I was doing the right thing. My only anxiety—about how Eva would cope—quickly disappeared as she immediately (within one month) started dating a man whom she subsequently lived with and married. This was a great relief, as I didn't have to feel guilty about her living alone.

As for my daughter, Maria, who now preferred to be called by her middle name, Theresa, Eva and I agreed that we should each have her 50 percent of the time. Thoughtlessly, we then abused Theresa for the first six months by moving her between our homes every two days. It never occurred to me that moving Theresa so often could be such a stress. When Theresa complained that she didn't want to go to school and tried to act sick, I dismissed this behavior as normal childhood complaints. It wasn't until January, when her kindergarten teacher said that Maria seemed unhappy, didn't socialize very well, and should be doing better than "B" work, that I came to the realization that Theresa was very unhappy and I had ignored her feelings.

When I realized what we had done, I was depressed. I felt angry at myself for not realizing that we had overlooked Theresa's feelings. We were so concerned with what was best for us that we presumed it would also be best for Theresa. Thereafter, I resolved to do what was best for her, even if I didn't like the consequences, and to listen to and observe her behavior for signs of unhappiness. Just to recall this mistake makes my heart ache for the unhappiness we caused her without being aware of it. I had followed my mother's example of ignoring her children's feelings. I realized that parents will automatically follow their own parents' example, as this is the only way they know, unless they make a conscious effort to change this automatic behavior pattern.

To rectify the problem, I immediately took her out of school and kept her at home with me for three weeks. I told her mother that this was necessary because Theresa needed to have one home as a base to feel secure and not be shuttled between the two. I also persuaded Eva that it would be best to change Theresa's schedule so that she would see the child only on weekends. Eva didn't object, because she knew Theresa had a preference for being with me and Theresa wasn't completely happy with Eva's boyfriend, with whom Eva now lived. Furthermore, I think Eva didn't object because she was reacting to our separation by turning most of her attention to her new boyfriend. Instantly, I knew I had done the right thing, because Theresa became very happy, singing all the time and asking me every day if it were true that she didn't really have to go to school and could just stay with me.

Seeing how happy she had become convinced me to have her start kindergarten over the next year and to alter my work schedule so that she was only in daycare from 10:00 a.m. to 3:00 p.m. This allowed me to devote substantial time to her, as well as giving her only one main household. We played together during this time, and I made self-esteem tapes for her, which I played for her every day. As I have since evaluated my life, this is the time I'm most proud of. The fact that I altered my life to help her before she developed serious problems is the best thing I've ever done. To this day, my daughter and I are very close; she is with me five days a week and we do many things together. She also excels at school and at most everything she does.

Even on the days she goes to Eva's house, I often see her at basketball or soccer games. Immediately prior to these games, we will meet so that I can work on her skills with her. After the game, we enjoy discussing the outcome. As a result, I'm one of the few high school parents who knows which students drink, including her, and she tells me about her social life in great detail.

\* \* \* \* \*

Now that I had separated from Eva, I decided that this was the best time to let out my old resentments towards my parents, so that I would feel totally free of all past negative feelings. I wrote my parents the following letter.

*August 14, 1983*

*Dear Mother and Father,*

*Please, be aware that this letter is written with the intent not to hurt you, but rather to heal myself. For approximately 20 years I have carried these resentments with me, and now I must cleanse my soul of these feelings. Deep down, I know they keep me from being truly happy and hinder my relationships with others.*

*Now I know that I've been taught and told I should grow up and learn to put aside these types of feelings, like you have towards your mother. However much I would like to agree with your suggestion of living with them, I can see that for me it doesn't work that way. All I have to* do is listen to the way you talk to your mother to know that you have never really gotten over your resentments. They obviously come out, as you have always tried to show her that you know more than she does.

So you see I don't want to follow your approach, because I don't want to treat you the same way. In fact, one thing is very clear—that until now, I have followed exactly the example you have set with your parents. It is time to break this family tradition.

Actually I have only one resentment—that my mother and father never took time to actually care for me or to love me. Of course, you were very good at giving me gifts and spending money; however, this isn't day-to-day loving. For instance, the basic need all people have is just to be heard. You have asked questions, but I know my answers were seldom heard. For example: If I was asked a question at dinner, you would never remember my answer the next day. Sometimes I intentionally told you different answers two days in a row to see if you noticed the difference. I can honestly say you never did! This didn't make a teenage boy believe there was any sincerity in his parents.

I soon became very frustrated at attempting to talk about my problems. I believed that the only thing you cared about was what kind of parents you appeared to be to others. I didn't have to tell you anything about me or what I really thought, because if everything appeared okay, you would never think of asking how the person inside was.

*It seemed that all you ever wanted was for me to appear successful so you could tell everyone of my success and they would think you were great parents. It seemed very important for you to appear to be great parents, and I learned that I must be very nice and controlled in public to project the image that you wanted of the nice family. But what did you ever know of me or my feelings?*

*You know I played football, but all I felt was that I could never be the superstar father wanted me to be—or rather the superstar he always wanted to be.*

*Did you know that I also played varsity baseball and I had games for two years? I don't believe you ever attended one and you seldom showed any interest.*

*Did you know that I had two varsity sports banquets at my high school, De La Salle? You must have known, because I remember telling you about them, but you had better things to do. Once you were at home drinking beer. Each year, I received a major sports award, and it was a very empty feeling to receive the award and not have anyone there who cared.*

*I could go on, but I hope you understand how I believed you only cared about things that affected your image as parents. As a result I obtained good grades, played football, and learned to be strong and independent, not trusting or loving or giving to others.*

*As for physical affection, I've been very surprised over the years to learn that mothers and sons actually hug and kiss and show affection. Now I realize that my upbringing was abnormal, and I'm still trying to learn how to be* affectionate towards others. I'm not sure I'm doing very well.

If you complain that I don't care or show you affection, you are right. It is a habit I'm trying to overcome, but it is very natural for children to follow their parents' example and the way they were taught.

I might have been able to forget these resentments, but over the years, nothing seemed to change. I felt you still only wanted everything to appear okay, and you were satisfied with this. I never felt you took time to discover how I felt about my life. For example, my wedding in Austria: I remember thinking, prior to the wedding, that there was no way you would come. I knew it would be inconvenient for you and, of course, cost too much. I was right. Other things you did could never make up for your nonattendance unless you had a good reason for not going. When people asked me if you would attend, they were shocked when I truthfully told them that it was too expensive and inconvenient for you.

Of course, prior to my wedding I remember living in your house and being treated poorly every time you drank. Some of the lines I heard were:

"You'll never go to law school, you're not smart enough."

"You can't make it through law school without my help."

"I'll take your car away from you [age 22] if you don't listen to me."

"Your girlfriend is a slut."

Those were some of the nice things said to me while you were under the influence. I always thought that if you had just said, "Sorry," it would be all right. Of course, I don't think you were sorry, because you believed you were right. You just forgot that I had feelings, but then again, you never knew what my true feelings were.

My law school graduation party was nice, but I know it was an attempt to make up for not attending my wedding and to show that you had a son who graduated from law school. This may be a very cynical view, but it is based upon the prior track record.

Now you have an idea of my feelings. I'm sorry they exist, but I'm attempting to deal with them. Please don't misunderstand me to say that I'm blaming you for anything that has happened in my life. Anything that I've screwed up in my life I take full responsibility for. No one is perfect, and we all have to deal with something from our parents. All I want to say is that we don't have a good relationship now. It lacks genuine caring and concern. Perhaps we should all learn how to be more caring and understanding. Let's not judge each other so much and accept the different ways we live. It's just that I couldn't do that until I cleared the air on my side.

It's my hope that you don't take this letter and deal with it as I've seen you deal with other things. That is because when you are hurt, you sit around and talk about it until you can justify that it is me who screwed up. No one side screws up any relationship. I know I'm equally to blame. Do you know the same?

John

> P.S. If you don't already know, Eva and I no longer live together.

Afterwards, my parents felt very bad, but *my* attitude changed, as I felt free to love them because there were no resentments holding back my emotions. Since then our relationship has improved, and I wish I had done this earlier. Our relationship could still be better, but I can accept its shortcomings because I've told them my feelings. One of the lessons I've learned is that resentment can eat away at a person and keep that person from being free to love. Constantly, I remind myself of this and often force myself to initiate discussions of any bad feelings I have to clear them out of my system. I discovered that a person cannot be happy if he holds resentment. I believe illness and disease seldom strike the truly happy person.

# 10

## *Marriage the Right Way*

Now that I had cleared my system of disease-causing emotions, I felt confident I would never again get cancer as long as I listened to my body. Listening to my body, I would know whether I was eating improperly, suppressing emotions, or under stress. I resolved to be happy.

One of the benefits of my illness was that I discovered how strong my inner power was. Through my visualization technique for fighting cancer, my will power strengthened to the point where I now believe that I can have anything I visualize. In Western society it could be called the power of positive thinking, and Eastern philosophy would say that I was in touch with the universal flow of energy, enabling me to attract what I visualized. Whatever name you want to call it, I believe that if I visualize exactly what I want or wish to accomplish and believe in it 100 percent, it will happen.

In other words, when I decide I want something, I set in motion a chain reaction that brings it to me. For example: In July, 1985, I decided to visualize a home in the country, with at least five acres, within 30 minutes of my office, and which would require a very small down payment, since I only had $7,000 in the bank. Every day, I told myself it would happen, and I let this belief remain in my mind without doubting its inevitability.

One Sunday, about three weeks later, I was driving home when I suddenly got the feeling I should exit the freeway. So I pulled into a gas station and noticed a real estate office. As you can surmise, I went into that office and, after telling an agent what I wanted, he immediately took me to a three-bedroom home on nine acres that had been on the market one year earlier and hadn't sold and was now back on the market. Three days later, I submitted an offer, not doubting that my bid would be accepted, even though another offer was pending that was slightly better than mine. My offer was accepted on terms which only required me to put $3,000 out of my pocket because the seller believed that I was a better risk to her than the other purchaser. I believe the seller came to this conclusion because her real estate agent was very impressed with my Mercedes, which I had bought in Germany for only $9,000, and the fact that I was an attorney. After all, any attorney with a Mercedes must be rich. I had two stereotypes working in my favor to make it appear I had more than $7,000 in the bank.

About a year later, I decided that I wanted to purchase a small apartment building, so I could achieve an early retirement. I visualized the building, including not having to spend more than the $20,000 I now had saved. One week later, I asked a builder who came into my office about apartment buildings, and he said he was just finishing a new nine-unit building which he was selling for $450,000. Generally, in a commercial loan transaction, one has to put down 30 percent, which would have been $135,000 in this case. Since I didn't have the required down payment, he was willing to work with me to obtain a bank loan. The result was that for $15,000 I bought this new building which had a $200-a-month positive cash flow. Right behind this building, the same builder was building a twelve-unit complex with a sales price of $650,000. When I inquired about that one, he said he already had a buyer. Nevertheless, I visualized that I would get it and eight months later, when the construction was complete, his buyer suddenly changed his mind. We again worked together, so that for $13,000 cash down I could purchase a new twelve-unit building with a $900 positive cash flow. I never doubted this would happen.

Another time, I decided I wanted to meet my real father, whom I last saw in the parting scene described in Chapter One. Previously, I had never been curious about my father, but now that I had had cancer I became more curious about my heredity and family traits. So I began to visualize meeting him, even while my mother and relatives said that they had no clue as to his whereabouts. Accordingly, I wasn't surprised when my uncle sent me my father's phone number and address in Texas. At my grandfather's funeral, an old friend of my mother's who knew my father had given my uncle the information.

I phoned my father and, after a general conversation, I decided to visit him, so I flew to Texas for the weekend. It was a very intense weekend, meeting my father for what seemed like the first time. I was touched that he still had a photo album of my first two years which he kept in his dresser drawer. It was the first time in my life that I ever met another male who resembled me in his actions and mannerisms. I felt much more whole and normal.

That night in Texas, I had a dream that completed a childhood memory. I remember sitting in the back seat of a car with my new fire engine, while my mother was in the passenger seat. A man was driving, but I could never see his face. When I was young I asked my mother who the driver was, and my mother said that it was my stepfather; somehow I was never convinced. I asked my father about the incident. He said that when he came back from California to Detroit to try to reconcile with my mother, he had bought me a fire engine and that he was the driver. That night I had a dream about the memory and at the point the memory had previously stopped I now clearly saw my father turn around and smile at me; I remember feeling deliciously happy but quickly looking down, as I felt very shy.

Through this dream I realized that I had been deeply hurt by the divorce, and I had buried memories of my father and didn't even acknowledge he existed. Since then, I have had many more recollections about my father. The one big regret I have is that my father has made no effort to continue, or perhaps to begin, a relationship with me.

The experience of having cancer and feeling close to death put me in contact with a part of myself I had previously ignored. Not only were my visualizations successful, I also received ideas or communicated with others not in my presence. A good example involves my dog, Fox, who had been with me for 13 years. I often joked that he was my longest lasting relationship. One Fourth of July he ran away when the fireworks frightened him. For two weeks he was lost, until one Monday morning, I awoke and knew he was ten miles away in another city's dog pound. I told my daughter and went to get him. He was there and scheduled to die in twelve hours.

One night, five months later, Fox became very sick and that night in my sleep, about 5:00 a.m., I had a dream where he was standing in the air with no background around him, just looking at me, very sad. He stared at me for a long time and then I woke up frightened because, though I presumed I was dreaming, it didn't seem like a dream. I couldn't sleep anymore, and when I went outside at 7:00 a.m. Fox was dead on the garage floor. He had come to say good-bye.

I don't believe that there is anything unusual about these types of feelings or powers, but simply that most people aren't aware that they have them. If people were more in tune with their internal bodies and believed in these ideas, more people would have these experiences.

Another experience I had that involved visualization and sudden knowledge or inspiration was in meeting my current wife. I had been single for three-and-a-half years, and I realized, while on a one-month trip to Japan and Taiwan with two Chinese women, that I had a lot in common with many Oriental women. Asian culture has a rice diet with little meat and a Buddhist philosophy with which I felt in tune. My visualizations, holistic living principles, and daily practice of Tai Chi were accepted and understood by them as normal.

Tai Chi is a Chinese martial art that is a combination of ballet and yoga. The practitioner does a nonstop, 25-minute dance in slow motion while concentrating on his breath. Its purpose is to promote health, happiness and harmony. Tai Chi is to be performed in a relaxed manner, and what amazed me about Tai Chi is that, after practicing for six months, I noticed that my arm muscles had become strong. Previously this had only happened when I did sports that required use of my arm muscles, like swimming. When I asked my Chinese teacher how this could happen, he just smiled and said that Tai Chi improves the circulation of chi, thereby strengthening the entire body. Chi is a special energy within everyone that can be stimulated through proper breathing. It is what gives the martial arts master his great power.

So I decided to visualize meeting an Oriental woman who had been born in Asia but who had lived long enough in the U.S.A. to be somewhat Americanized. A couple of weeks after starting this visualization, a girlfriend told me that I should place an ad in the newspaper for an Oriental woman. She said that I was obsessed with them and she thought she would only have a chance with me if I got Oriental women out of my system. She even recommended a local newspaper, *The Weekly*, that specialized in personal ads for professionals and business people. I had never read this paper and about a week later, when I saw a copy at an old girlfriend's house, I examined it. Much to my surprise, there was this ad.

*She is 31, a bright, attractive, considerate, and generous Oriental professional woman. She enjoys music, the arts, movies. She has traveled a lot and she's learning photography for more travel. She also enjoys camping, snow and water skiing, and is just starting to understand American football rules. She wants to meet a patient, understanding man who she can share her thoughts and feelings with and do the above things together with. Handsome, nonsmoking, gentle and considerate man who doesn't mind having an Oriental lady friend, please write. Reply ad #1084, The Weekly.*

*August 21-27, 1985*

It sounded like a possibility, so I tore the ad out and put it in my sports coat pocket. It wasn't until about a week later that I answered, after I found the ad in my pocket while at work. Here's what I wrote.

*Dear Ad #1084,*

*I'm a blonde, bearded, handsome male who prefers Asian women. Recently I just returned from Japan and Taiwan and plan trips to China, Japan and Nepal within the next year or so. My preference is for Asian philosophy and it is reflected in my lifestyle. I practice Tai Chi daily, and I enjoy eating Japanese and Chinese food. I don't smoke and I eat a healthy, non-meat diet. I'm 36 years old.*

It sounds like we have a lot in common, and I suggest we arrange a lunch date.

Until then,

John

P.S. This is the first time I've ever read The Weekly; perhaps it is fate.

About ten days later, on a Monday morning while shaving, I suddenly knew that today I would meet a special woman. It was one of those intuitions I had started unexpectedly receiving since having cancer. Nevertheless, when I got to work, I was very busy and completely forgot about my inspiration. At 12:00 P.M., Miss April Han phoned to say she was responding to my letter. My reaction was one of surprise, since I had no expectation that my letter would be answered. However, even then I didn't associate Miss Han with my intuition. I did suggest we go to lunch immediately so that we could meet and end any expectations and false hopes. She agreed, and as I drove to meet her I only hoped it wouldn't be an unpleasant experience. However I, rationalized that, if she was a disappointment, it would only be for a one-hour lunch.

Much to my delight, our lunch was very enjoyable, and her smile and shy mannerisms were very captivating. She was from Korea, and had studied to become a CPA. She had been in the U.S.A. for seven years. In fact, she arrived in Seattle two days after I had moved here from Detroit. A CPA friend of hers had met his wife through the personal ads and had written this ad for her.

So one thing led to another and, two years later, I suddenly realized I was ready to get married for the right reasons. For the first time in my life I no longer suffered from "the grass is greener" syndrome. Now I could look at other women, know they were attractive, but realize I wouldn't be happier with them. They couldn't make me laugh everyday as much as Myung (her Korean name) and she was always so pleasant to be around that I no longer longed for that perfect woman who must be waiting just around the corner.

In fact, this idea was one of the themes of our wedding—a wedding that we totally planned and that was done our way. I was determined to absolutely make up for my first wedding and do it right.

We had the ceremony outdoors on our nine-acre parcel under several giant evergreen trees, with flowers all around us. We invited a small group of friends who received the following invitation:

*Myung Sook April Han*
*and*
*John Robert Wagner*

*request the honour of your presence*
*as they begin their voyage*
*with the ongoing mission*
*to continue to share*
*happiness and love*
*to go where*
*few other couples have gone before*
*on Saturday, the fifth of September*
*nineteen hundred and eighty-seven*
*at one o'clock in the afternoon*
*15203 Manor Way*
*Lynnwood, Washington*
*Myung Sook and John*

My two brothers, my parents, and my good friends Vince and Lynn came to the wedding. We sought to be serious, but with a lighthearted touch that reflected our interest in humor. This theme ran throughout the ceremony. My good friend Dick began the ceremony by reading the following story, taken from the book, *Secrets,* Chapter 5:

At that time, in the land of people, lived two teddy bears; one male, one female. These two teddy bears lived far apart but were united by the same goal—to read the secret words which were written in the peak of the magic mountain. It was said that whoever read these words would attain happiness. Many had attempted the journey, but few had returned. Because both teddy bears had an overwhelming desire to know the secret for happiness, they set aside their fears and set out on their quest.

When the first teddy bear arrived at the mountain, she observed many others attempting to climb. They all wanted to obtain happiness, but the few that survived departed in failure. She was determined not to fail, so she sat at the foot of the mountain to contemplate how best to attain her happiness.

When the other teddy bear came to the mountain, he immediately tried to assail to its peak. Repeatedly he failed, but each time he began again. As long as he survived, he would never give up his quest.

One day after he failed again, he met the first teddy bear sitting patiently at the foot of the mountain. He asked her what she was doing, and she replied, "Preparing for happiness." He said, "Don't you know there is only one way to attain happiness? That is by reading the secret words." She said, "No, happiness is not something to be conquered or found in one certain place. It is a special feeling inside you that comes from joining together in the challenge of going onward and always upward, in the sharing of the opportunity to have much more because two have joined together."

With those words, she reached out and took his hand. He then knew what she knew, and they set out together.

This was the last time they were ever seen.

However, legend has it that there are two teddy bears living on the mountain peak, and that these words are written there;

"This mountain is named happiness, and it can only be attained though freedom—the freedom of Love."

When Dick finished his reading, Myung Sook, who had sung as a teenager on Korean radio and who secretly fantasized about being a rock star, sang "You Light Up My Life" by Debbie Boone. No one there had known how well she could sing, and this romantic song produced a lot of tear-filled eyes. I then followed by doing what I do best, attempting to be funny, and I said the following:

"I could tell we had a lot in common because of the things we did together. For example:

"When we met, she didn't like 'Star Trek,' and now she loves it! Of course it doesn't matter that we had to see 'Star Trek IV' four times. The important thing is we did it together.

"Another example is playing poker. At first she said that she hated gambling, but now she thoroughly enjoys it and it doesn't matter that she only plays with my money. What's important is that we do it together.

"Of course she also decided to do Tai Chi; what's important is that we do it together, not that she does it better after one year than I do after three years! What is important is that we have decided to accept the challenge and opportunity to have more and have joined together."

When I had finished, my daughter Maria Theresa, stepped out and said, "I now pronounce you man and wife."

Finally, eleven years later, I had done it right and we had gotten married our way. I didn't do anything I didn't want to do. The slate was wiped clean.

We followed this with a Korean ceremony, complete with Korean attire. What most men will relate to is that the woman makes three promises to the man. The first is that she gives me her body; second, she vows to give me her spirit; and third, she vows to give me all of her. In return I say, "I accept." This is quite in contrast to the traditional American ceremony where the women say the final "I do" and always have the last word. (Joke—no letters please!)

Throughout the Korean ceremony there is an emphasis on traditional meanings and values that all the guests found very interesting. I thoroughly enjoyed myself and felt like I believed a person should feel at his wedding.

When the ceremonies were over we changed clothes, played volleyball and later that evening, poker. It was our day and we did it our way.

# 11
# Winning the Lottery

At the beginning of the last chapter, I described my real estate visualizations. What helped fulfill those visualizations is that my law work totally involves real estate and I understand how to acquire property for very little down. So when I came upon the properties through visualization, I already knew how to make them mine.

About three years after I had acquired the two apartment buildings, which were back-to-back, I became aware that there was a condominium shortage in Seattle and condos were selling at fantastic prices. So I decided to legally convert my apartment units, which were all two-bedroom, two-bath units, into condos. I estimated that the units which I'd bought for $50,000 each as an apartment unit had become worth approximately $115,000 each as a condo. This would give me a profit of $1,361,000 minus selling costs. Who wouldn't seize such an opportunity?

So I immediately started the conversion process and in two months had all the units ready for sale. I had even gone so far as to pay my tenants $700 each to move out, because it is easier to sell vacant units. Unfortunately, Seattle's real estate market, which had been on a one-and-a-half year boom cycle, suddenly came to a total stop. At the first open house, not one person came to view the units, and during the first month there was not one single offer. During this time, my monthly payment was $10,000, and I had paid all the tenants to vacate. Smart move!

Feeling financially threatened, I called upon all my real estate knowledge to help me. First, I realized that my units were nice, but nothing special. Therefore, there was no reason a buyer would prefer my units over someone else's unless I gave him a reason. The reason had to be a lower price with great terms. Fortunately, other sellers found it hard to accept that the market wouldn't suddenly improve because they had counted on the paper profits that were there just two months prior. So when I lowered prices dramatically, other sellers were slow to compete because of their hope (or greed) for greater profits.

At first, I lowered the prices to $99,950 and six weeks

later, to $89,950. I offered to carry a contract for as little as $6,000 down, with nine percent interest (when the going rate was over ten percent.) Luckily, over the next four months I sold all my units, and though I didn't end up with any cash, I did receive monthly payments of over $12,000. I felt like I had won the lottery!

But Myung Sook remembers the stress and the many options I had to continue to work on. I personally was responsible for a third of the sales through my own marketing efforts, and I had to refinance my house and make some fancy maneuvers to obtain $500,000 financing to pay off the bank loans on the building so I could sell the condos on contract. Nevertheless, the end result of all my efforts was … I had won the lottery!

It took all my real estate knowledge to turn this into a success, and it still requires my attention, for I have had to take four units back and handle their resale. In one particular case, the U.S. government seized one of the units and arrested the owner, claiming he was running an escort service out of the unit. The government refused to pay the monthly payment and told me that I would have to wait until the criminal case was resolved before anything would happen—a period of at least a year.

I found this unacceptable, and I started foreclosing on the federal government. I was really just bluffing, and I knew this might be a fruitless act, but the government had seized five other properties from this defendant, and I threatened to challenge the government in court and alert the other owners (of the other properties they had seized) that they could fight back—another bluff. Much to my surprise, the government suddenly dropped their claim to this unit and let me foreclose on the owner. I felt bad for the other owners, who didn't know they could challenge the government, which acted as though all their activities were proper and you had no chance against them. Two years later, the case was still going on, and I felt sorry for the other owners whose property was still tied up.

# 12
# Conclusions...And Then?

Now that I have finished with the "Ripley's Believe It or Not" sections on visualization, I have a few thoughts to offer in conclusion. The purpose of this book was to try to illustrate how my own decisions and personality traits contributed to my getting cancer and, conversely, how any person can take control of his or her life and find happiness through tragedy.

In other words, I believe everyone must take personal responsibility for their lives and accept that everything that happens to them results from their actions. When I accepted this fact, life became very simple, as there was no need for excuses nor to blame anyone. I can always see now how I had played a significant part in any unfavorable outcome in my life.

As a result, when people ask me if I believe nutrition is important to good health, I tell them that there is no doubt in my mind that the lack of it contributed to my getting cancer. I ate a very poor diet—without vegetables, heavy in sugars and junk food—prior to developing cancer, and logically it had to have weakened my immune system. I don't need a scientist to tell me this, because now all I have to do is eat something bad for my system and my body tells me. However, when it comes to recommending a specific diet for someone, I can't do that.

Everyone must take responsibility for their own health, get in touch with their own bodies, and find the diets that are right for them. I've tried most diets—macrobiotic, raw foods, wheat grass, "Fit for Life"—and had good results on all of them. However, my body is always changing and I've yet to find one diet that feels right all the time. Periodically my body says, "Change your diet." There are certain basics I abide by, like not eating salt, sugar, canned food etc.; but I'm always changing my diet within this framework.

When it comes to medical advice, health food advocates want me to say that I rejected Western medicine. To me this is foolish, because I don't believe in rejecting or not using something that has some success. As a result, I go to Western doctors, Chinese herbalists, naturopaths and chiropractors, depending on the ailment. For example, if I have severe pain or infection, I would go to a medical doctor for diagnosis and treatment to relieve the pain. Then when the pain has been relieved, I would go to a Chinese herbalist or naturopath for additional help, because I believe Western medical doctors mainly treat symptoms and the other healers are better able to help me eliminate the root of the problem. In other words, being sick is a signal for me to reevaluate my life in all aspects to find the cause of the problem. I ask myself, "What has my diet been like?" "Am I happy or under stress?" "How can I change any problems I have?" This is what I did when I had cancer, and if I had been satisfied with the advice and treatment given me by my medical doctors, I don't believe I'd be as healthy and happy as I am today.

I'll never forget them telling me that the things I did couldn't have helped, just because they hadn't read in a medical journal that my techniques passed a double-blind scientific test. Years later, I've read that the American Medical Association now says that beta carotene, which is found in carrot juice, can help prevent cancer, and that fiber in the diet can have the same effect. I'm glad I didn't wait for their approval before I started my dietary changes. In terms of treatment, they are starting to use new techniques that attempt to stimulate a person's immune system to fight cancer. Couldn't it be that some of these cancer diets and visualizations could have the same effects?

A story I like to tell involves my daughter, Maria Theresa. Over a period of a few months, she kept having pains in her abdomen. One day we were out walking when she suddenly curled up on the street clutching her stomach, in extreme pain. I immediately took her to a medical doctor, fearing a serious problem. The doctor's examination found nothing wrong, but he sent us to the hospital for further tests. A couple of hours later we were told there was nothing wrong and sent home. The next day I took her to a Chinese herbalist. He looked at my daughter's face, and before I could tell him why we had come he shouted, "Gas, very severe gas problem, look at face, color wrong and too puffy," I couldn't quite see what he saw, but the Chinese believe that the condition of the internal organs shows up on the face. He gave us some herbs, and within two weeks her gas pains disappeared. It was a relief to find a person who recognized the problem. The doctor's tests didn't show a problem, therefore the doctor said there was no problem. Tell that to my daughter when she is lying on the sidewalk.

Another illustration involves my wife, Myung. Seven months after we had our first child, I became aware that she had an increased heart rate. This resulted in her not being able to sleep at night because her resting pulse was 115. We went to her medical doctor, and she immediately conducted a test on her thyroid. The test results indicated that she had a super-active thyroid, a condition known as

Graves' disease. The doctor indicated that unfortunately this was not an infection in which the thyroid would heal itself, and there was no known cure for Graves' disease. The doctor recommended radioactive drugs which kill the thyroid to control the problem. The doctor stated that after the drug therapy killed the thyroid, Myung would have to take hormones the remainder of her life to regulate her heart rate.

At 35, this seemed a radical procedure, and we immediately sought another alternative. First, we went to our naturopath, who said that he had successfully treated other patients with the same diagnosis. He gave her herbs and suggested she return every week while the problem was acute. He felt it was an infection, even though the medical tests indicated otherwise.

In addition, we went to a Chinese acupuncturist, who said that this problem was probably a result of childbirth and was very treatable. He recommended acupuncture every week, and we immediately began treatment.

About one week later, Myung's pulse—which at the highest point was 115 at rest and 140 walking around—dropped to about 100 at rest and 120 walking. A week later it dropped to 94 at rest and 105 at walking around. It continued dropping until it returned to normal.

Her medical doctor's reaction was one of surprise. She concluded that it must have been an infection. Of course, if we had followed her advice, Myung's thyroid would have been inactive and she would have had to take hormones the remainder of her life. What her doctor didn't tell us was that there are often other problems caused by killing the thyroid. Ask the former President's wife, Barbara Bush, about her eye problems.

This was a case in which it was very tempting to follow the doctor's advice. At night I'd listen to Myung's heart beat when she had been lying in bed, and it was frightening to hear it beating so fast and hard. I feared she would have a heart attack at any moment.

I had asked the doctor about my fears, and she said that this wasn't likely. We did keep a prescription handy that lowered the heart rate if it went much higher. Fortunately, we didn't need it and we were able to save her thyroid through natural means, using Western medicine as a backup if needed.

Another question I'm often asked is whether it is satisfactory in maintaining good health just to be without stress? My answer is that everything in the world and our bodies is connected. Stress is a component, but so is our physical and spiritual health. To stay healthy and happy, a person must be in harmony in all aspects of their life.

Another question I'm often asked is whether Eastern philosophy is better than Western philosophy or religions? I don't have an evaluating system to determine which is better, but I seek to obtain benefits from all philosophies. In many respects, I see great similarities between East and West. I only know that if I can maintain a relaxed state of body and mind through proper diet, exercise and stress control, I feel happy. When you just relax, good things will follow. Live each day as though it is your last and you will realize how unimportant most things are.

With that in mind, you'll have a better chance to take control of your life. I now have a very successful law practice in which I only work five to six hours per day. Of course, I could make more money by working more, but I enjoy walking in the woods, playing with my daughters, coaching a girls' soccer team and having a close family. These things are most important to me, because I'm always aware that I could die at any time.

If I told you that you would die in two years, would you continue to live as you do now? If not, get control of your life. Take responsibility for everything that happens to you. Don't blame others. Believe and work to attain what you want. Live your life your way. I always identify with Frank Sinatra's song, "My Way." If I can change my life, anyone can. Just recall all the stupid things I did that I related to you in this book, and it should be obvious that I'm no one special, yet I managed to change. So can you!

# 13

## *Life Insurance*

It was 1993, and I finally decided it was time to do estate planning. Though I'm an attorney, I did not have a will nor the necessary trusts with which to protect my assets. I was always too busy with other projects to take the time to do estate planning. Even though I had nearly died, I still believed I wouldn't die suddenly, but would have an adequate warning to do proper planning. Does anybody ever learn?

In any event, I consulted with an insurance agent. This agent attempted to place coverage for me, but, surprisingly, encountered a difficulty. Insurance companies considered my type of cancer terminal. I found this very distressing, because this wasn't the way my oncologist had explained it to me. What about my 30 percent chance to survive? When I phoned Dr. Weber, he didn't want to talk about my numerical chances of survival, but rather to focus on how well I was doing. He even said that he would mail me an encouraging article on myeloma.

True to his word, the doctor sent the article. It was a bombshell. The title was "Long-Term Clinical Course," and it included a summary stating that the survival rate was 85 percent at ten years. This was the most encouraging part, and I suspect that the doctor never read the article. One of its conclusions was, "Multiple bone involvement appears to be inevitable in solitary plasmacytoma of bone, given enough time." Overall, every patient in the study had had a second occurrence within ten years, and 60 percent within five years, but those patients with an "M" component (which I had) had a four times greater chance of a local recurrence within five years. This article supported the proposition that my cancer was terminal, even though it had an initial slow rate of growth.

This was not the encouraging article Dr. Weber thought it was! After the initial shock, I was able to take solace in the fact that, even though I had the "M" component, I had surpassed everyone in their study. Nevertheless, it was not pleasant to read that all studies considered me terminal.

What this article did do was reinforce my belief and hope that I was doing something right, since my case surpassed their best patients' case histories. However, my cancer fears were inflamed because, over the last three years, I felt my health had slightly deteriorated.

There were three reasons for this fear. One was that I had developed an unknown stomach problem. For unexplained reasons, I would suddenly get stomachaches, approximately three times a week, that could become very intense regardless of how carefully I ate. I had gone to a homeopath, an acupuncturist and an herbalist—even a medical doctor, who did an ultrasound of my stomach and gallbladder. The doctor didn't find anything wrong. The homeopath gave me something that worked for a month but was ineffective thereafter. The acupuncturist/herbalist refused to do acupuncture on me because, he said, I had yin deficiency and a damp heat problem; by treating one with acupuncture, I would make the other one even worse, because they were opposite problems. He treated me with herbs for a year, from which I had some improvement. He gave me good tips, like not consuming cold food or cold drinks, which were known to trigger bad stomachaches. However, my stomach problem still hadn't satisfactorily resolved, and he told me I would have to live with it and be very careful of my diet.

The second problem which concerned me greatly was that even though I was eating the perfect low-fat diet, my cholesterol was 270 with only 35 HDL ("good" cholesterol), when the average male had 45 HDL. I tried everything to lower my cholesterol and raise my HDL. I tried increasing my exercise from one hour to one-and-a-half hours per day and taking garlic capsules, fish oil capsules, Niacin (which I had to discontinue because *it* upset my stomach), and oat bran. On one occasion my cholesterol dropped to 190, when I ate 100 mg. of oat bran per day for an entire month. Unfortunately, I couldn't continue eating this much oat bran. And there was no way I would consider the cholesterol-lowering drugs, because the long-term side effect was liver damage.

My third problem was that I had started to get a cold and the flu every year, after not having had either for ten years. I wondered if my immune system was becoming weaker, though I knew I might be overreacting since these illnesses were of a short duration and I now had small children around, increasing my exposure.

Nevertheless, I had a subtle fear that something wasn't right, and the insurance companies and my doctor's article fanned the flames. My conclusion was that it was time for me to visit Dr. Gonzales.

Dr. Nicholas Gonzales is a medical doctor whom I had read about in *East-West Journal*, now called *Natural Health*. He has developed and expanded upon the Kelley cancer program, a metabolic approach. I was attracted to Gonzales' program because it was similar in many respects

*We have a copy of Dr Kelly's questionaire to determine body types*

to the Gerson program I originally undertook. Not only did it include coffee enemas but pancreatic enzymes, which, some research studies show, efficiently fight tumors. Dr. Gonzales was compiling case studies and had recently been funded by the National Cancer Institute for a pilot program. I had sent my sister-in-law to him after she developed breast cancer for the second time, and she was doing well two years after the new cancer had been discovered. I had been impressed by her program.

I made an appointment with Dr. Gonzales immediately after he agreed to take my case. (He will not take patients who have had extensive chemotherapy or who lack the commitment to do all that the program entails.) Three weeks prior to my visit, I sent the blood test results that he had requested and scalp hair samples. At the appointment, he conducted a complete physical.

The results of his analysis were very startling. He began by explaining to me that 80 percent of his patients were placed on some type of vegetarian diet. However, one of the tenets of his program was that everyone had a different metabolism and everyone's program was varied to match their metabolic need. His results indicated that I was in a small minority group of his patients whose diets should include organic meat. He compared my metabolism to that of an Eskimo, or lion or tiger. He stated that if you took a lion off meat, he would die prematurely.

I was shocked, and felt threatened at having my lifestyle abruptly changed. I had grown to be very comfortable being a fish-eating vegetarian, and I related to the philosophy of vegetarians. However, I had to admit that some of the points he made were exactly right. For instance, he asked if I enjoyed meat. I had to admit that I had had a lifelong craving for meat. Prior to giving it up (for 13 years), I couldn't imagine a lunch or dinner without meat. Second, he asked what fish I liked. My answer was "especially salmon and halibut, and that lately I could eat salmon every day." He said this fit into a meat-eating pattern, because these were big-flesh fish, and the fact that I also reported I hated most whitefish and small fish further indicated a meat-eater. In addition, my strong desire for fish indicated my attempt to compensate for the lack of meat.

The topper to all this was that he believed eating meat could lower my cholesterol over a long period of time. His theory was that my liver was continuing to produce excess cholesterol because I didn't provide it with other cholesterol. My body needed the fat in meat to function more efficiently. However, he made a big point that hormone-free and grass-fed beef were greatly preferred over regular supermarket products.

In addition to this dietary change, he had done a metabolic evaluation that provided a numeric rating for 49 of my organs and systems—my digestive, respiratory, cardiovascular, nervous, lymph and endocrine systems. In addition, he had analyzed levels of about 40 vitamins and minerals to determine deficiency. Based upon these results, Dr. Gonzales designed a supplement program to fight cancer and improve my body's efficiency. As a result, I take abut 100 supplements a day that range from adrenal gland, lung, lymph, and liver to the basic vitamins and minerals.

He also determined my cancer risk numerically. My number was 12, with a higher number having a greater risk. His typical patient averaged about 28. Any number under 10 was good, with 1-5 being the goal of all patients. Any number over 20 placed a person in great danger of having cancer.

Even though my number was not excessively high, I decided to do the program because I felt I needed a tune-up. I had no idea how long my number had been at 12, but I suspected it had gone up recently. So for peace of mind, I decided to commit to the program.

So in addition to the supplements, I also take four pancreatic enzymes four times a day on an empty stomach, at least one hour before or after meals. Dr. Gonzales believes that there is abundant research to show that pancreatic enzymes can break down tumors. This part of the program is essential, and Dr. Gonzales goes so far as to regulate the source and production of the enzymes because only active, organic enzymes are going to produce the desired results. For most patients with active cancer, he requires them to wake up in the night to take four pancreatic enzymes so that they maintain a constant supply in their bloodstream around the clock.

It is interesting to note that Gerson, in his book, uses pancreatic enzymes to aid digestion, but this is one essential difference between the two programs. Gonzales believes in and uses pancreatic enzymes to break down tumors. The other essential difference is that Gerson places everyone on the same vegetarian diet. Gonzales does a metabolic evaluation to determine each person's dietary needs. Though most patients are placed on some type of vegetarian diet, everyone's diet varies somewhat. For example, one person may be told to eat white fish twice a week, while at the other extreme there is a small minority like myself for whom Gonzales recommends eight ounces or more of organic meat per day. Likewise, your metabolism determines how much and which juices you should consume daily.

A very important part of the program that Gerson and Gonzales agree upon is the daily need for coffee enemas. Their only disagreements on this point is which side it is better to lie on while doing the enemas, and whether it is necessary to use the external colon tube. (Gerson opposed it.) Gonzales has his patients do at least two consecutive enemas twice a day. To detoxify the liver is the goal of both programs, and these enemas are to be done in full every day.

Gonzales has his patients cycle off the supplements for five days after every fifteen days of taking them. This is to further aid detoxification, and Gonzales has to continually remind patients that they are not going backwards during this five-day period.

On every other "off" period, there is a designated procedure to promote detoxification and removal of poisons from the body. There is the liver flush, clean sweep, and others which I have attached as supplements (see page 139-146). What is significant is that as great an emphasis is placed on detoxification as on nutritional intake.

One of the reasons I was committed to the program was that I feared my health was deteriorating because of the frequent stomachaches. When I visited Dr. Gonzales, I had had a stomachache for two days. Upon considering my problem, he offered the simple explanation that I was dehydrated. This was difficult to believe, since I drank large quantities of vegetable and fruit juices and herbal teas. Dr. Gonzales explained *only water cures dehydration.* As to tea, it can make one more dehydrated. He recommended that I drink at least six glasses of water every day between meals. It should not be tap water, carbonated, or juice-flavored seltzers. He said he had one case of a lady with asthma for nine years who was cured after drinking eight to ten glasses of water per day for three days. He feels that many cases of ulcers and asthma can be greatly improved by drinking water and that at least 60 percent of Americans suffer from dehydration.

Skeptical as I was when I left Dr. Gonzales' office, I bought and drank noncarbonated mineral water. Within three hours, my stomachache was gone. Nonetheless, I didn't quite believe it so simple; but two-and-a-half years later, I can confirm that this is the case. I daily drink the six glasses of water, and on the few occasions I start to get a stomachache, I immediately increase my water intake and the problem subsides. However, I've noticed that cold water or cold food can immediately *cause* stomachaches when taken on an empty stomach.

The aspect of the Gerson and Gonzales program that I've received the most questions about is coffee enemas. I wish there was a scientific method to prove they detoxify the liver. I think they work, and I offer two examples.

The first involves my father-in-law, who is 75 and had Hepatitis C for many years. This means he himself didn't have the symptoms but carried the disease. Everyone had to be careful not to eat or drink after him. When I became aware of this situation, I suggested he try the coffee enemas and he agreed. After two months of daily enemas, he was examined by his medical doctor and pronounced cured. This doctor told him he had never had heard of or seen anyone cured of this illness. When my father-in-law told him about the coffee enemas, he said there was no connection and that coffee enemas were dangerous. I related this story to Dr. Gonzales and he said that he regularly treats cases of hepatitis in this manner. It usually takes six to eight weeks for a cure.

The other story involves my brother-in-law, who was told by his doctor that his liver function was very poor. He started the coffee enemas, and one month later, his doctor told him his liver had greatly improved. Interestingly, my brother-in-law's cousin, who was opposed to coffee enemas, was so shocked by how my brother-in-law's physical appearance had changed after doing the coffee enemas that she has started doing them, too.

It is my belief that, at the very least, coffee enemas provide me with a form of life insurance, and I need all the coverage I can get.

This may be the only life insurance policy a cancer patient can obtain. Regardless of the treatment course a cancer patient follows, I believe you shouldn't overlook doing everything possible to improve your health. If your body makes new cancer cells, you want to be fully armed to physically, emotionally, and spiritually win the battle. Cancer is not a dread disease whose outcome is dependent on your doctor's treatment. *It's your battle.* **You can win.**

# Interview with Dr. Nicholas Gonzales

*[In this interview, questions from John Wagner are indicated in boldface type. Responses from Dr. Nicholas Gonzales are in plain type.]*

**Do you call your approach to cancer the metabolic approach?** Well, I don't really, but other people call it that. I'm simpler than that, I just use nutrition. It is called metabolic. To be honest with you, it's not a term that I like, and I don't particularly use myself; so when people ask me what I do, I say it's just nutritional therapy.

To me, everything is metabolic; even chemotherapy is metabolic. Every drug or nutrient is going to involve metabolism, so I don't like that term, although people use it all the time.

**What happens to the typical patient who comes to you?** I always tell people, to sum it up quickly, it involves three basic things: diet, supplements, and detox. The uniqueness about this program is that we don't have one diet; we have ten diets, and all kinds of variations, and they range from pure vegetarian (nuts and seeds) to red meat group two to three times a day, and all gradations in between. Using the blood work and our hair test we evaluate which specific diet the patient needs to be on.

The supplements vary from patient to patient, too; it's all individualized. As you know, they go on vitamins and minerals. And the main thing for cancer is the pancreatic enzymes. And the average cancer patient takes a fairly heavy dose of pancreatic enzymes, which we believe have a direct anticancer effect. Studies go back to 1902 to demonstrate that, so it's not our idea that pancreatic enzymes fight cancer. The first paper was published in approximately 1902.

The third part of the program involves detoxification, which are just simple techniques which help the body get rid of metabolic and stored waste material, dead cancer wastes and that kind of thing. They include coffee enemas that help the liver work better, liver flushes, juice fasts, and a whole variety of techniques that simply help the body get rid of metabolic wastes, which for cancer patients we believe is very important.

**How does the hair analysis work?** Well, we measure about 100 different biochemical parameters of the hair. We computerize them; it's just an assessment of the status of the patient in terms of their biochemistry and physiology. It's just a kind of computerized extrapolation for biochemical information.

**What kind of success rate have you had?** For compliant patients, it runs that around 75 percent of all our cancer patients get well. Twenty-five percent don't. Most of our cancer patients are pretty advanced when they come to us, but the majority of them get well.

**And do most of the patients go on a vegetarian diet?** No, it's about maybe 40% on the vegetarian side, 30% balanced, and 30% meat-eating. So it's about a 40-30-30 split. By the nature of my practice, most of the patients I see end up on a vegetarian diet, but it is fairly evenly divided.

**So what is your background and how did you get into this program?** I'm trained as an immunologist., but my research interest in medical school was nutrition. When I was a second-year medical student, under the then-head of Sloane-Kettering, I began to investigate the work of Dr. Kelley, who was the man that was aggressively using pancreatic enzymes in a nutritional program to treat cancer. I spent five years, ultimately, in a formal research setting, going through thousands of his records, trying to document the effectiveness of his treatment. We put that together into a monograph as part of my immunology training research requirement—a 500-page monograph—where we reviewed literally hundreds and hundreds of his patients. The results are revealing—hundreds, thousands of patients

**So you didn't expect to find the results that you did?** Well, I was very skeptical when I started, but we quickly found that the enzyme therapy seemed to be quite efficacious. We got complete medical records and interviewed the patients; we tracked them very, very aggressively. There were patients with aggressive advanced cancer who five to ten to fifteen years later were still alive and obviously, or apparently, disease-free. It was quite an interesting experience.

**So far, what has been the traditional medical community's response to this?** Well, initially, I think they were hoping I'd get hit by a low-flying jet plane, but in recent years it's completely changed. We've gotten funding to do three clinical trials; we're in the middle of a pancreatic clinical trial right now which probably will conclude in about a year. We've just been funded for a metastatic colon cancer and a metastatic lung cancer trial, and we're just starting those trials right now. So very shortly we'll have three fully funded, fully academically supervised clinical trials in operation. So I think there's increasing support ... a lot of good support from the academic world. And the data from the studies has demonstrated what the program can or cannot do.

**And the program is working with the patients in the study?** Yes, the pancreatic study is going beautifully. The majority of patients, most of whom had just months to live, are doing extremely well. The first patient we entered is now out to two years and seven months, and she had about three months to live. Pancreatic cancer, when it's inoperable ... usually the immediate survival is about three months to six months. So the patients on it are already doing well.

**Is there any type of cancer patient you would refuse to take?** Well, if a patient can't eat, they can't do the program. You know, if they've had half their gut taken out in surgery, they can't do the program. We find patients that have had bone marrow transplants, they've had so much chemo and radiation sometimes, it's just not going to work for them. Sometimes the amount of previous therapy is the limiting factor. We can treat patients who've had chemo, surgery, and radiation, but there comes a point where, if they've had ten different drugs over three years and lots of radiation, we're not going to succeed. So the practical issue is, can the patient eat and do the program? Because they have to do it at home. Are they strong enough to do the program? And how much radiation and chemotherapy have they had?

**Have you ever given thought to combining your program with other programs, such as Simonton's?** I think Simonton's work with meditation, visualization, and relaxation is important. I always say that getting well isn't just taking nutrition—it's nutritional, psychological, and spiritual. Getting well is 100% nutritional, 100% psychological, and 100% spiritual. So all these are really important. A lot of patients would like to make it just nutrition, but that's not really what's involved in getting well. I think things like the Simonton approach are really quite valuable, and I think it's a good adjunct. So I think patients should look into those type of things.

**Have you found that your program works with any other type of illness?** Well, we treat everything from multiple sclerosis to rheumatoid arthritis to chronic fatigue, and it seems to do well for most of these things, most of the time.

**Have you tried any AIDS work?** I have a couple, literally two, patients with AIDS, though it's not really something I'm an expert in. But I have a couple of patients that are followed by their immunologist, and I put them on the nutrition program, and they're doing fine; but it's too soon to tell and I certainly don't have enough experience with HIV. Although clearly, I think good nutrition would be far more helpful than bad nutrition, I just don't have enough experience with it; I've really concentrated on cancer.

**How important is it, do you think, for people to eat organic food and drink non-tap water?** I think it's critical. I had a patient who was using tap water in their enemas, and their cancer markers kept getting worse until they changed their water. Clean food is critical. If I don't eat organic food myself, I don't feel well. Patients have to really try to keep their environment and their food as clean as possible.

**Is there anything else you can tell me?** No, I think you've covered a lot of ground. Basically that we've doing clinical trials, that we're trying to prove what it can do by academic standards, that we've gotten funding to do the trials, and it seems to do very well. The trials will ultimately demonstrate just how good it is.

**I appreciate your taking this time. I think it will give people more hope. And let's add your address and phone number, so people can reach you if they're interested:**

*Dr. Nicholas Gonzales*
*36 E. 36th St., Suite 204*
*New York, New York 10016*

*(212) 213-3337*

# Appendix: Detoxification

These detoxification routines are taken from the non-published materials of Dr. Nicholas Gonzales.

## The Coffee Enema

Coffee enemas have been used for over a hundred years as a generalized detoxification procedure. Despite rumors to the contrary, coffee enemas are perfectly safe when taken as directed. Coffee enemas stimulate the liver and gallbladder to release stored toxins and wastes, and this enhances liver function.

Unless otherwise specified, we recommend each patient take the enema each morning and afternoon.

We usually recommend patients prepare a quart of coffee, using 2 tablespoons of coffee grounds per quart of water. The water should be purified with the reverse osmosis filtration unit; if you do not have such a unit, store bought spring water will suffice. Of course, organically grown coffee is best for this procedure.

The coffee should be made in a stainless steel or glass coffee maker. Aluminum is not recommended, since aluminum is a toxic metal and can leach into the coffee while perking. You should add one tablespoon of unsulfured blackstrap molasses to each quart of coffee, while the coffee is hot; the molasses aids in retaining the enemas and also increases the efficiency of detoxification. It is acceptable to make the coffee the night before use; this allows the coffee to cool. The coffee is best used at body temperature. If it cools too much overnight, reheat slightly before using.

When preparing to take the enema, lie on your left side and lubricate using KY jelly or similar substance. Insert the colon tube slowly about 12-18 inches into the rectum; if it kinks, pull back and try again, as kinking will block flow of coffee.

Release the stopper, and let about a pint of coffee slowly flow in, then reclamp. If the coffee won't flow, this usually means there is a kink in the rube, and you must withdraw the colon tube and reinsert. At first, it may be difficult to retain the enema, but we usually recommend holding the coffee about ten minutes before expelling.

Repeat the enema, holding for another ten minutes. You should do two doses, each consisting of one pint, held for ten minutes, in the morning, and two doses in the afternoon between 2 p.m. and 5 p.m..

At first, you may feel slightly jittery, although most patients find the enemas relaxing. Usually, the jitteriness lessens after about the third session. If the jitteriness continues, this means you are making the coffee too strong.

## *The Purge*

The purge is one of the most important detoxification routines for cancer patients. The purge puts the body at rest and aids the rapid removal of metabolic wastes from the body. In addition, the purge pushes the body into an alkaline state, in which repair and rebuilding of damaged tissues occurs rapidly.

First, make a punch consisting of the following: Juice of 6 grapefruits; Juice of 6 lemons; Juice of 12 oranges

Do not include the peel. Put the juice from the above fruit into a gallon jug and add purified water until the jug is full.

Upon arising, drink one tablespoon of Epsom salts dissolved in half a glass of purified water. One-half hour later, take another tablespoon in half a glass of water. In another half-hour, take of third dose of one tablespoon of Epsom salts in half a glass of water. You will now have taken three doses over a one-hour period.

Approximately two hours after the first dose of Epsom salts, take a glass of the citrus punch. Thereafter, take a glass every hour. You are to eat no food that day except, if you wish, an orange for dinner.

You should take one capsule of Acid Calcium three times during the day, spread out through the day.

During the purge, you may feel a variety of symptoms, such as nausea, headaches, muscle aches and pains. Such symptoms indicate the body is mobilizing stored wastes, and should not cause alarm.

On day two of the purge, repeat the above.

## *Additional Detoxification Routines*

1. *Salt and Soda Baths.* During periods of intense toxicity, a warm bath with added baking soda and salt can greatly help to mobilize toxins out of the body through the skin. In a fairly warm bath, add one cup of baking soda (sodium bicarbonate) and one cup regular table (or sea) salt. Lie in the bath for 20-30 minutes. The bath should be repeated daily until symptoms diminish.

2. *Mustard Foot Soaks.* This particular remedy is very helpful for toxic headaches, generalized "goopy" toxic symptoms, muscle aches and pains, and water retention in the ankles or other parts of the body. In a basin of very warm water, add one tablespoon of prepared mustard and a teaspoon of cayenne pepper. Sit in a comfortable chair and soak your feet in the basin for 20-30 minutes. The soaks can be repeated two to three times each day, and should be continued during periods of intense toxicity.

3. *Castor Oil Compresses.* These compresses are particularly useful when applied to areas of pain, or where tumors might be breaking down. Buy castor oil from your health food store. Warm the oil *gently* in a pan. Soak a washcloth, towel, or other natural cotton cloth in the oil and apply to tumors, areas of pain, and areas of inflammation. Keep the compress in place for 60-90 minutes. You can place a hot water bottle on the

compress to keep it warm. The castor oil poultices can be applied as often as you need relief, as they are not harmful. Do be careful not to overheat the oil, or you might burn yourself when applying the compress.

4. *Skin Brushing.* Skin brushing is a method of stimulating and cleaning the lymphatic system and detoxifying the skin. However simple it may seem, it is a *very powerful*, effective technique. Use a long-handled brush, with natural vegetable bristles; the brush should be kept dry. The body should be dry, and the brush should be passed over the skin in a clean sweeping motion—no back-and-forth or scrubbing motions. The brushing should be done in the direction of the lower abdomen—up the legs, up the arms, and down the neck and trunk. The face should not be brushed. Skin brushing should be done once or twice per day. In times of intense toxicity, the brushing can be increased to four times per day.

## *Clean Sweep Protocol*

Materials: Intestinal Bulking Agent II (Holistic Horizons) Organic apple or tomato juice.

Add one *level* teaspoon of Intestinal Bulking Agent II to 8 ounces of juice. Shake or stir to mix thoroughly in a jar of shaker, then drink immediately (mixture will solidify if allowed to sit).

Follow with an 8-ounce glass of water.

Repeat this three times a day for five days, for a total of fifteen doses. During this procedure, follow your prescribed diet, but take the doses away from meals. Continue your coffee enemas daily.

When you have finished the Clean Sweep, resume your supplements and eat yogurt two or three times a day for the next five days to replenish your bacterial flora. We recommend only brands with active cultures.

The bulking agent can absorb many times its weight in

water and in the gut, enlarges much as a sponge does when exposed to water. The swollen mass gradually works its way through the small and large intestine, filling every nook and cranny and forcing out all manner of stored wastes that would not otherwise be excreted.

During the procedure, you may feel discomfort the first day or two due to the expansion of the bulking agent in the intestinal tract. This is a good sign, and means the bulking agent is stretching the intestines to maximum diameter.

Most patients on this protocol pass a variety of exotic particles and substances. Many describe passing long casings, similar to a snake skin or sausage casing, that actually represent dried mucous and dead cells from the surface of the intestines. These wastes can accumulate over a period of many years and seriously interfere with the absorption of nutrients.

This procedure is also the most effective way, in our experience, of removing abnormal bacteria and other organisms from the gut that often take hold after antibiotic use.

## *Management of Hemorrhoids*

The soft, inside part of the banana peel has a powerful bioflavonoid that is an effective treatment for hemorrhoids. The use of banana peel to treat hemorrhoids is actually an ancient folk remedy from Africa.

Use only the soft material from the inside of the peel. Scrape this off and apply to the affected area twice per day. A pad can be worn on the undergarments to prevent staining.

For a less messy approach, take the soft inner material from the peels of one or more bananas and roll small amounts in your palm to form cylindrical pellets. Put the pellets on a plate, cover with waxed paper or a plate, etc., and put into your freezer. The frozen pellets can then be inserted into the rectum like suppositories. Before inserting, we suggest you warm the pellet slightly in the hands and then insert into the anus. They can then soothe the affected area from the inside. Use the suppositories twice per day.

## Nasal Irrigation

Nasal irrigation with saline is very helpful for patients with sinus problems and allergies. We suggest the use of the Narial Nasal Irrigator. This small porcelain container makes irrigation of the nose easy and neat.

The directions for irrigating the nose are included with the irrigator. Put ¼ teaspoon of salt with warm water in the irrigator and use as directed.

## Cleansing the Skin

The body uses four main systems to excrete waste materials; the liver and the intestinal tract, the kidneys, the lungs and the skin. Too often, we forget that the skin can be used to help detoxify the body and speed the removal of metabolic waste. On our program, cancer breakdown products and other metabolic debris tends to accumulate rapidly, and often our patients develop all manner of skin eruptions and blemishes. Such conditions may be worrisome, but should be viewed as a good sign.

Once a week, rub your skin from head to foot with a mixture of equal parts of olive and castor oils (the castor oil is available at any pharmacy). Then, with the oil still intact on the skin, take a hot bath for fifteen minutes. The bath allows the oil to penetrate to the deepest levels of the skin. After the bath, go to bed under heavy covers for one hour to sweat out the poisons. Be careful getting in and out of the bathtub—the oil will make you slippery. Finally, take a hot shower.

The oil soaks should be done weekly for the first three months of the program; at that time, they can be discontinued.

## *Liver Flush Protocol*

Materials:
1 gallon apple juice
½ bottle of Phosfood (Standard Process)
Acid Calcium (PSI)
Epsom salts
Whipping cream and berries
Olive oil
Bentonite liquid

1. Add one-half bottle (one ounce) of Phosfood to the gallon of apple juice, and shake. Over the next four days, drink the full bottle of juice. (This usually breaks down to about 3-4 full glasses a day, best taken between meals.) Be sure to rinse your mouth out with baking soda or brush your teeth after drinking the juice to prevent the acid from damaging the teeth. While drinking the apple juice, eat normally. Take your coffee enemas as you normally would throughout the procedure.

2. On the last day of the procedure (the day after you finish the apple juice), take two capsules of Acid Calcium immediately before breakfast and two capsules of Acid Calcium immediately before lunch.

3. Two hours after lunch, take 1-2 tablespoons of Epsom salts dissolved in a small amount of warm water. Add juice to cover the taste, if desired.

4. Five hours after lunch, take one tablespoon of Epsom salts dissolved in warm water. Add juice if desired.

5. Six to seven hours after lunch, eat a dinner of heavy whipping cream and fruit, as much as desired. Any fruit is acceptable; patients generally prefer a mixture of berries, either frozen or fresh. The mixture of fruit can be blenderized to make a shake. With dinner, take one Acid Calcium capsule.

6. One-half hour before bedtime, drink ¼ cup of bentonite liquid.

7. At bedtime, drink ½ cup olive oil. A small amount of orange, grapefruit, or lemon juice may be added if desired.

Immediately after finishing the oil, go to bed and lie on the right side with knees drawn up for 30 minutes. You may feel nauseated during the night, due to the release of stored toxins from the gall bladder and liver. This is normal and will pass. To us, it is a good sign, because it means the procedure is working.

      8. On the next day, eat normally. Take two Acid Calcium capsules with breakfast, two Acid Calcium capsules with lunch, and one Acid Calcium capsule with dinner.

      The liver flush, in a simpler version, was first used during the 1920s as a means of improving liver function. The procedure we recommend is a refinement of the original technique and serves several important functions. First, the orthophosphoric acid helps remove calcium and lipids (fats) from arteries, and normalizes cholesterol metabolism. The phosphoric acid, working with malic acid found in apple juice, also dissolves and softens gallstones. The magnesium in the Epsom salts relaxes the sphincter of the gallbladder and bile ducts, allowing for easy passage of the softened, shrunken stones. Finally, the cream and the oil cause a strong contraction of the gallbladder and liver, forcing out stored wastes, bile, and stones which easily pass into the small intestine. These wastes and stones are then excreted. We have found that the liver flush is a simple way of removing gallstones without surgery, while at the same time lowering cholesterol levels and improving liver function.

# BIBLIOGRAPHY

Cousins, Norman. *Anatomy of an Illness.* New York, W.W. Norton, 1979.

Gerson, Max, M.D. *A Cancer Therapy.* 5th ed. Bonita, CA, Gerson Institute, 1990.

Holmes, Thomas H. and Richard H. Rabe, "The Social Readjustment Scale," *Journal of Psychosomatic Research,* 2 (1967): 213-218.

Simonton, Carl O., M.D., Stephanie Matthews-Simonton, James L. Creighton. *Getting Well Again.* New York, Bantam Books, 1978.

Walker, Norman W. *Diet and Salad.* Phoenix, O'Sullivan Woodside & Company, 1971.

## ORDER FORM

| Qty. | Title | U.S. | Canada | Total |
|---|---|---|---|---|
| | *Thirty and Terminal: Cancer Survival* | $12.95 | $15.95 | |
| | Subtotal | | | |
| | Shipping and Handling (Add $3.00 for one book, $1.00 for each additional book) | | | |
| | Washington residents only, add $1.06 sales tax per book | | | |
| | Total Enclosed | | | |

**Payment Method: Please Check One**

❏ Check (Payable to JOHN R. WAGNER)
❏ Money order

❏ **Credit Card Orders:**
   Expiration Date: _____/_____
   Card #: _____
   Name on Card: _____
   Signature: _____

❏ MasterCard    ❏ VISA

❏ **FAX Orders:**
   1-206-363-9607  Fill out the order blank and fax.

❏ **800-Number Orders:**
   1-888-363-9500
   Have your credit card number ready

*Please send to:*

NAME _____
ADDRESS _____
CITY _____
STATE _____  ZIP CODE _____
DAYTIME PHONE _____

### JOHN R. WAGNER

11231 Roosevelt Way N.E. • Seattle, WA 98125

Quantity discounts are available.
For more information, call 206-363-9500
***Thank you for your order!***